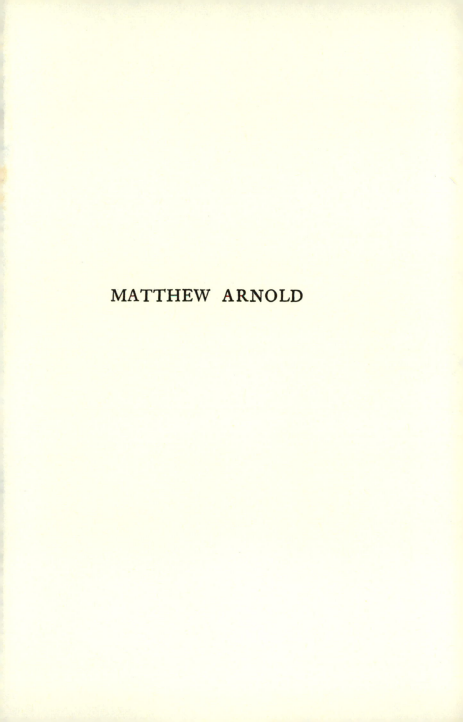

MATTHEW ARNOLD

MATTHEW ARNOLD

A Critic of the Victorian Period

BY

CHARLES H. HARVEY

ARCHON BOOKS
1969

First published 1931
James Clarke & Company, Ltd.
Reprinted 1969 with permission
in an unaltered and unabridged edition

SBN: 208 00732 6
Library of Congress Catalog Card Number: 69-18273
Printed in the United States of America

PREFACE

THE biographers of Matthew Arnold have a difficult subject. His family life can be seen in the two volumes of his Letters, edited by Mr. George Russell, and in Mr. Russell's book, published by Messrs. Hodder & Stoughton, Ltd., 1904. These contributions by Mr. Russell are important, owing to his close acquaintance with Arnold. But since the publication of Mr. Russell's selection of the Letters, additional and most important Letters have from time to time appeared, in particular Arnold's correspondence with Cardinal Newman; and with Swinburne, for which the public is indebted to the Literary Supplement of *The Times;* and to Mr. Arnold Whitridge's " Unpublished Letters of Matthew Arnold." Then there is the survey of Arnold's work by Dr. Garnett, in the Dictionary of National Biography.

Single volumes have appeared dealing with some one aspect of Arnold's many-sided work. Professor Saintsbury gave the literary judgment of a very great critical master. Mr. Herbert Paul was especially valuable on the political side. Mr. W. H.

Dawson made a careful study of Arnold's ideas, especially from the German side, but his book lacks the vital interest of actual accomplishments, and Arnold, with all his airy manner and his poetry, was a moving force. Sir Joshua Fitch has described Arnold with the authority of an educational expert. Then there are a number of smaller separate studies, in every case a beautiful tribute to his influence, such as the little volume of the Rev. Arthur Galton, and " Appreciations," by Francis Bickley and Mr. A. F. Kelso.

To the many reviews it is impossible to refer, but those by Lord Coleridge and Lord Morley caught some of the light from Arnold. We must, however, draw special attention to the unique Bibliography by the late Mr. Thomas Burnett Smart. This is indispensable to the student of Arnold. It is a model, and a most effective description of the immense influence of Arnold on English life. Arnold was in life a worker, and much of his writing is the direct effect of realities working upon his mind.

Further light upon Arnold's personal character came in 1902, when a selection from his notebooks was published by his daughter, the Hon. Mrs. Wodehouse, later Lady Sandhurst. Arnold's notes for every fifth year, from 1863 to 1888, and all those between 1852 and 1861 were given.

No one can really understand Arnold without a

PREFACE

knowledge of these notebooks. Through them can be seen in reality that the word " Culture," so often on his lips, was indeed the master word of his practice; and above all it can be seen that the great critic of Victorian life was the austere critic of his own life, and pursued perfection with monastic severity.

The present writer has attempted to combine the foregoing material and to set forth the comprehensive range of Arnold's influence, for rarely has a single mind touched modern life at so many points with such disturbing force. As we recede from the last century, and its historical features become clearer, we see that Matthew Arnold, inside the Victorian era, was the Victorian critic. It is this internal view of the Victorians which is now presented to the reader.

The proofs of this book have been read by Mrs. F. J. Harvey, and, while the Author takes full responsibility for the statement of facts and opinions therein, he desires to acknowledge with gratitude the help that he has received from her critical judgment in questions of expression and presentation.

CHARLES H. HARVEY.

1931.

CONTENTS

MATTHEW ARNOLD

An Outline of His Life

THE deep importance of heredity is shown so vividly in the history of the Arnolds that the writer takes this to be the true starting point in studying the genius of Matthew Arnold. Up and down we see in the genealogy of this family a remarkable manifestation of power and accomplishment.

Matthew Arnold's father was the great Dr. Thomas Arnold, Headmaster of Rugby School. His place in English education is known. So powerful a personality must have created an ideal atmosphere for the development of his children. It has been said that there was not great sympathy between the Doctor and Matthew. Matthew's references to his father are full of affectionate respect but are not overwhelmingly plentiful. Yet there are distinct resemblances between them. Toleration, originality, the moral insistence, style, the sense of history, the close relationship between idea and practice, all these were characteristic of both. Can they be traced further back ? First, on his father's side. Thomas Arnold's mother was Martha

Delafield, who married William Arnold (died 1801).
Along this line we are referred back to Irish sources,
Fitzgeralds and Dillons among the Delafields, and
to a Suffolk family near Lowestoft before the 16th
century.

Then, on his mother's side. Mrs. Arnold was
Mary Penrose, and along the Penrose line we find
two clergymen, and further back Devonshire
families of Ford and Chudleigh. But we see no
outstanding names. Mrs. Humphry Ward has
suggested Celtic origins in the names Fitzgerald
and Dillon, and points out Celtic features; and in
a letter to his mother, referring to his visit to
Brittany in 1859, Matthew says that the Breton
peasantry reminded him of " dear Tom and Uncle
Trevenen," with " their expressive, rather mournful
faces, long noses, and dark eyes." (" Letters,"
Vol. I, p. 85.) Mr. G. W. E. Russell, a close friend,
suggests that the Arnold ancestors may have been
Jews who emigrated from Germany to Lowestoft,
where Arnolds lived for several generations. But
of this there is no proof. His portraits certainly
have a Jewish expression, and we may refer here to
the great sympathetic friendship with the Rothschilds
in his middle life.

In another direction there was much in Arnold,
especially in his poetry, which points to Celtic
connections. The distant ancestry is unknown.
But we have full account of the life in which

Matthew was nurtured, and this we now give.
Thomas Arnold, in 1818, at the age of twenty-three,
was ordained deacon at Oxford.   In 1819 he
settled at Laleham on the Thames, near Staines,
with a brother-in-law, Mr. Buckland, in a school
preparatory for the Universities. This same school
was transferred under the name of " Laleham " to
Bexhill in 1911.

In 1820 Dr. Thomas Arnold married Mary
Penrose, the daughter of the Rev. John Penrose,
Rector   of   Fledborough,   in   Nottinghamshire.
Matthew was born on December 24, 1822. No
notice of the event appears in Dean Stanley's Life
of the Doctor, although there is a good deal at this
time about Grecian and Roman History, and the
Rev. John Keble's hymns.   Keble, it may be noted,
was Matthew's godfather.   The family life at
Laleham in these first years of Matthew Arnold had
the true Arnold characteristic—quiet happiness and
peaceful development.   Lord Coleridge has described " a bright little fellow put upon a table before
a roomful of people at Laleham and reciting with
intelligence and effect a passage of Burke."   And
Arnold himself refers in one of his letters to " where
I used to play with my brothers and sisters, and walk
with the governess, and bathe, and learn dancing
and many other things." (" Letters," Vol. I, p. 20.)
In 1828 the Doctor moved to Rugby, that Rugby
founded by a grocer, for his great work as Head-

master of the school. The family went by coach the whole way, Matthew a boy of six. Matthew returned to Laleham as pupil of his uncle for a time, but his boyhood from now onwards was spent for the most part in the surroundings of the Arnold family life, as they have been described in Dean Stanley's Life of the Doctor. For the greater part of the year he was at Rugby, and in the vacations, after 1833, at Fox How, a house in the valley between Ambleside and Rydal, in Westmorland. Dr. Arnold had built Fox How with the money coming to him from the sale of his father's property in the Isle of Wight.

Fox How became the centre of the Arnold family. It appears prominently in the Doctor's Life, in Matthew Arnold's own letters, and later in the next generation in the work of Mrs. Humphry Ward and the Right Hon. H. O. Arnold-Forster. The whole family looked to Fox How as its central meeting-place, and it has become indissolubly attached to the great literary and public works of the Arnolds. At Rugby, then, and Fox How, Arnold's boyhood was spent. At Rugby he had the school atmosphere; and the record of his father's great achievement there suggests the powerful influences bearing on him.

At Fox How, on the summer visits of the family after 1833, when he was eleven years old, Matthew came into contact with Wordsworth and the dying glories of the Lake School, dying since S. T. Coleridge left for London. Hartley Coleridge was still at Nab Cottage, a few yards away. Robert Southey was at Keswick. There are a few references to these in Matthew Arnold, but Wordsworth was the great influence. At Rugby, the pupils of the Doctor, so many destined to become great names, Clough, Stanley, Hughes, were, of course, contemporaries and associates of Matthew through the Doctor.

But what of the Doctor and Matthew ? It has been said that there was not much sympathy between them. Let us see the facts. There cannot be a more lovely picture of happy family life than that of the Arnolds. " Rugby Chapel " is the sufficient expression of a son's love and reverence. But there are scores of intimate pictures of the interior Arnold life, such as that in which we see Matthew singing the Rugby Confirmation Hymn. Grave schoolmaster as he was, Victorian as Mr. Strachey places him, he yet was a sound, hearty Englishman, loving walks, hunting and outdoor life, a child with his children. But Matthew went to Winchester and then to Balliol, and the natural Arnold independence asserted itself.

There are very many traits of the Doctor in his son, in expression and in principles, and especially in a general, unconventional view of things, but there is one vital difference between

them.   The strict—shall we say, puritanical—atmosphere of the Doctor's home, and the fearful
Tractarian storms which so occupied the Doctor's
mind, allowed but little scope for the humour which
in Matthew was irrepressible.   Through the whole
course of Dean Stanley's Life there is not the
slightest touch of humour.   But the natural
Victorians were not humorous; it was the critics of
the Victorians who were humorous.

It is clear, however, that Matthew Arnold owed
many dominants in his character to his father.
And Matthew Arnold's " Letters " contain many
acknowledgments of this debt.   Indeed, some
passages from Dr. Arnold have the very ring of
Matthew.   Here is one in which the Doctor must
have copied his eight-year-old son: " I must
write a pamphlet on the holidays or I shall burst."
(Letter, Nov., 1830.)   " Business ought not so to
master us as not to leave time for a better business."
(Rugby, Sept. 17, 1832.)   Or, take the letter on
his treatment of Prophecy (July 28, 1835).   This
letter is perfect Matthew Arnold.   Or this to Mr.
Justice Coleridge: " But the whole thing makes me
most earnest that we should soon meet, not to argue,
but rather to feel the many points of true sympathy
between us, and to get our notions of each other
refreshed, so to speak, in all their totality."   That is
the very tone of Matthew.

To his mother's influence Matthew Arnold

always referred with reverence and with love. His letters are fragrant with frequent acknowledgments of his mother's care, and her bringing up of her children, so unworldly, so sound and so pure. At fourteen, Matthew went to Winchester School, with another brother, under Dr. Moberly. He was there a year, and entered Rugby School in August 1837, after a short tour in France with his father and mother and two other children. He was again in France with Dr. Arnold and his brother Tom in 1841. In 1840 he won a prize for Poetry at Rugby with the poem, " Alaric at Rome " which was recited on June 12, 1840. This was his first published poem; there is nothing of special interest in it apart from the first example which it contains of a most marked characteristic of his poetry, the repetition of a word in a conspicuous position.

" Yes, there are stories registered on high,
    Yes, there are stains Time's fingers cannot blot."

He won a Balliol scholarship in 1840 and went to Oxford on October 15, 1841, his father noting in a letter that this was the first separation of the family. So that with the exception of the year at Winchester he was under the direct influence of his father up to eighteen years of age. President Wilson said: " I used to say, when I had to do with the administration of an educational institution, that I should like to make the young gentlemen of the

B

rising generation as unlike their fathers as possible."
(" The New Freedom," p. 36.)   Did the Doctor
work towards this in his son ?   Much that Matthew
wrote would have offended his father, and yet one
can see the working of the same independence,
the same fresh treatment of old subjects, the same
instinct of attack and correction.

In 1841, at the age of eighteen, Matthew Arnold
was at Balliol, Dr. Jenkyns being Master. Benjamin
Jowett was then a young Fellow, and Mr. Lingen
(afterwards Lord Lingen) his tutor. Oxford was
in the heat of the Tractarian fight, but Arnold
apparently felt little interest in it. Later he described
his attendance at John Henry Newman's preaching.
Of his life at Oxford at this time the best and possibly
only account now known is Principal Shairp's
verses on Balliol Scholars, 1840-1843 (" Glen
Desseray and Other Poems "). Dr. W. C. Lake,
a private tutor to Matthew Arnold, thought there
was " an apparent want of earnestness in all his
work which made it difficult to see what he would
ultimately become."   This gives an outline of
Arnold which certainly shows him at a distance from
the Anglican controversies. At this time he was a
member of a small Debating Society called The
Decade. It was at first limited to ten members.
Some names are worth recalling; Jowett, Tait,
Church, John Duke Coleridge, Thomas Arnold,
Shairp, Conington, Chichester Fortescue, F. T.

Palgrave, Arthur Stanley, A. H. Clough. Fame has certainly thrown its net over that group. In October 1842 he won the Hertford Scholarship, and in the same year Dr. Thomas Arnold died suddenly. Matthew's particular friends at Oxford were Clough and Theodore Walrond, and with them and his brother he used to go up the Cherwell and along the river by Iffley and Sandford. It has been said that they had an arrangement to breakfast in Clough's rooms every Sunday morning.

In 1843, Arnold being twenty, he won the Newdigate prize with a poem, "Cromwell." It is to be noted that in the final examination for Classical Honours he won only a second class. In 1845, the year in which Newman went over to Rome, Arnold was elected to a Fellowship at Oriel—Clough, Burgon, Church and Fraser being contemporaries —where also his father had been a Fellow. These five years at Oxford set a permanent mark upon him, as much as he set a mark upon Oxford. How greatly Oxford entered into his life his readers know. We have only to think of " Thyrsis " and " The Scholar Gypsy " and the famous passage from the " Introduction to Essays in Criticism " to feel the charm of the city on him. Hence it is a matter for regret that so little has come down to us of his Oxford days. More recently some letters of Arnold have been published (*Times Literary Supplement,* March

31, 1921) which reveal the influence of Newman upon Arnold in a stronger light. Arnold wrote, November 29, 1871, to Cardinal Newman:

> " I cannot forbear adding, what I have often wished to tell you, that no words can be too strong to express the interest with which I used to hear you at Oxford, and the pleasure with which I continue to read your writings now. We are all of us carried in ways not of our own making or choosing, but nothing can ever do away with the effect you have produced upon me, for it consists in a general disposition of mind rather than in a particular set of ideas. In all the conflicts I have with modern Liberalism and Dissent, and with their pretensions and shortcomings, I recognise your work ; and I can truly say that no praise gives me so much pleasure as to be told (which sometimes happens) that a thing I have said reminds people, either in a manner or matter, of you."

The set of this influence started in these Oxford days. Dr. Arnold was steadily thinking of a profession for him, and apparently at first decided on Medicine, but Matthew did not like it. Apparently he studied for the Law, since—our authority is Prof. Saintsbury, " Matthew Arnold," p. 7—he was actually called. The Doctor disliked the Law. After receiving the Oriel Fellowship, Matthew took Classics in the Fifth Form at Rugby. Soon after this, in 1846, we see him, as he describes himself in the essay on George Sand, deeply occupied with George Sand's writings, and resolving to see the places of her work, and herself. He gives quite minute details of his journey to Berry, and his meeting her and Chopin; and from this backward glimpse of Arnold we see something of the social enthusiasm, something of the new light in Nature which then possessed him.

In 1847, at the age of twenty-four, he became Private Secretary to Lord Lansdowne, President of the Council in Lord John Russell's Government, thus being brought into contact with official education. Of his duties at this time little is known; one or two references in his letters show him with a kind of republican tendency somewhat curiously in contrast with the high surroundings of his office. He attended, for example, the Chartist Convention of 1848. Little is known of Arnold's external life between 1845-1851. He went to France; and reference to this has already been made. Some effects of this visit, and possibly of others, can be seen in his poetry. The series, " Switzerland," and all the poems dealing with the " Marguerite " subject are based upon his experiences during this period. This biographical blank, together with the love episode indicated in the " Switzerland " poems, give the starting-point for an objectionable suggestion recently made by Mr. Hugh Kingsmill. (" Matthew Arnold," Duckworth, 1929.)

It is said by Mr. Kingsmill that Arnold's correspondence, 1845-1851, was deliberately destroyed by Arnold's family in order to conceal his discreditable personal history at this time.   Incredible as it may seem, Mr. Kingsmill suggested that there was an episode of disgrace, that Arnold at Thun, in Switzerland, met a French girl, a governess-companion, living in apartments, of a lower social order than himself, and fell passionately in love with her.   Arnold is said to have seen her again in the second year, and then to have parted from her finally.   These suggestions are not supported by a single scrap of definite evidence.   They are simply imaginative translations of Arnold's poetry.

The world outside Arnold's own family knows little of his life between 1845-1851.   But what is known suggests other reflections than those of Mr. Kingsmill.   It was the birth-time of the finest flower of his poetry;   the majestic sonnet on Shakspere, the Sophocles sonnet, " Stagirius," and " Resignation."   The severe purity of the poetry of that period, its high thought, its Wordsworthian closeness to Nature, seem to place it apart from and above the human scene.

The present writer, at any rate, is unable to understand how any poet could treat the theme of Love without some human reference in his mind. It is an entirely natural thing to presume that even Arnold's passionless love-poetry must have had some human being to give it form and pathos.   The touch of the vanished hand, the sound of the still voice are poignantly there, and they may have been the hand and the voice of some real Marguerite. But what more ? What is the characteristic of this poetry ? Surely that it is divested of physical trappings and ascends in its sense of loneliness into a communion with Nature even more impersonal than Wordsworth's, more real than Shelley's, more penetrating than that of any Celt.

Soon after the defeat of Lord John Russell in the House of Commons, on June 14th, 1851, Matthew Arnold was appointed by Lord Lansdowne to an Inspectorship of Schools, and this position he held for thirty-five years, till 1886.

Shortly after his appointment to the Inspectorship he married, June 10th, 1851, Frances Lucy Wightman, " a dear and gracious little lady," third daughter of Sir William Wightman, one of the Judges of the Queen's Bench, and him he accompanied on Assizes as Marshal. Matthew's family appeared to have thought him unlikely to bear easily the yoke of marriage. But his letters and all private testimony confirm the happiness of his family life, and the picture presented by his letters is singularly beautiful, even for the Arnolds. Of Matthew's marriage, Mrs. Ward has given us Dean Stanley's opinion that it greatly improved him, he " retaining all the genius and nobleness of mind which you remember, with all the lesser faults pruned and softened down." (" A Writer's Recollections," p. 52.)

We now see him for some years travelling a wide district in this exacting, perhaps monotonous, work. His letters again and again show signs of impatience: " My wife and I had a wandering life of it at first. There were but three lay Inspectors for all England. My district went right across from Pembroke Dock to Great Yarmouth. We had no home. One of our children was born in a lodging at Derby, with a workhouse, if I recollect aright, behind and a penitentiary in front. But the irksomeness of my new duties was what I felt most, and during the first year or so it was sometimes insupportable." (Quoted in Geo. E. Russell's " Matthew Arnold," p. 48.)

But he had a strong sense of duty. His Reports have been published ("Reports on Elementary Schools, 1852-82") and are referred to in the chapter on his educational work. In some respects the work was congenial. He could indulge his liking for travel, although this separated him from home. His letters describe his life at this time, inspecting, travelling from place to place, and in the midst of it all, the steady work at Poetry, he producing in the intervals of this prosaic work, now by candle light, now in early morning, here, there, poem after poem of flawless workmanship. Is it to be wondered at that now and then there reaches us a barely suppressed cry of weariness at his occupation with the three R's?

Recognition comes; he is elected to the Chair of Poetry at Oxford. This Chair was established in 1708 under the will of Henry Birkhead, Fellow of All Souls, and carried a stipend of about £130 per annum. The High Church party had put up a candidate against him, but there was a majority of eighty-five for Arnold. The lectures were given in Latin, until Arnold broke away from custom and gave them in English. Indeed, Arnold began a new order by his tenure of the Chair, setting a fresh standard for his successors. Among his hearers was Swinburne, with whom later he kept up a friendly correspondence on literary matters and each sending the other volumes of his works as they were published. Unfortunately, a stray passage in the "Arnold Letters," published after Arnold's death, infuriated Swinburne, and admiration turned to hate.

Arnold wrote an account of how he went in the morning to Lowther Arcade to buy toys for his three boys and could " scarcely have found a more genuine distraction than in selecting waggons for Tom and Trev, with horses of precisely the same colour, not one of which should have a hair more on his tail than the other—and a musical cart for Diddy." In 1858 he moved to No. 2 Chester Square, and spent in Switzerland a holiday of climbing and bathing with Theodore Walrond, but without Mrs. Arnold, as he lovingly records.

In 1859 he was appointed Foreign Assistant Commissioner of the Commission presided over by the Duke of Newcastle, to report upon the State of Popular Education in England. He met Guizot in Paris, and Madame de Staël, and Sainte-Beuve and Ernest Renan. At this time the Continent was excited by the struggle between Italy and Austria, and Arnold expressed his sympathy with Italian independence in his first prose work, " England and the Italian question," 1859, a pamphlet which brought him into political notice at once. Reviews by the principal journals and communications from men such as Mr. Gladstone, show that his name already had power. His opinions as to French Military Superiority are all wrong so far as 1870 is concerned, but the letters of this visit are interesting. They show his keen increasing interest in public life, and his gradual ascent to public influence.

Interesting, too, is all his work of this time as containing the lines of his future development, and specially as showing how he seized hold of that border ground between educational work and political life in which he became such a sower of ideas. In 1859 the Alpine Club elected him as member. His military interest took a practical form in London when he returned, for he joined the Queen's Westminsters as a Volunteer, his idea being that by means of the Volunteers the upper and middle classes could become as superior in physical force as they were in wealth and intelligence.

The Report for the Commission occupied him for the next year and a half, together with his Lectures in the Chair at Oxford, afterwards published as " On Translating Homer," 1862. The Report was published in February, 1861—" The Popular Education of France, with notices of that of Holland and Switzerland, 1861." This work and the Oxford Lectures are sure marks of his developing individuality. Don't let us miss the perfectly natural life of family, children, holidays, relations in which he moved. Here is the seat of those sane, clear judgments which began to come with wonderful rapidity. The line of his activity was making itself clear. He was forty in 1862.

The output of writing was now very great. The Lectures at Oxford appeared in the volume, " On Translating Homer; " the report on his Continental educational tour; an article on the Revised Code controversy; the Crewian oration on " The Modern Element in Literature; " an article on Spinoza; one on Dean Stanley's Lectures; Dante and Beatrice; and then singly—almost monthly— the great series of essays, published together later as the first volume of " Essays in Criticism." Almost every line written during these years, 1861-1864, has become permanent literature, simply by the natural vitality of the ideas.

To assess the value of this writing, compare with it the torrent of stuff poured out in journalism, great then, infinite now, which disappears the day after publication. And yet this was the work of a School Inspector, done during the intervals of inspecting the three R's, writing in trains and railway station waiting-rooms. His letters of this period show increasing social engagements. At one dinner he met Geo. H. Lewes, Herbert Spencer, Swinburne, Browning and Ruskin. He wanted to be Master of Trinity, Cambridge. But even beneath the social distractions we see him planning work and really unhappy when not carrying it out.

At forty-one he feels himself growing older, but full of spirits and inward buoyancy. Friends multiply, such as the Rothschilds and the friendly circle of the Forsters—his sister married Mr. W. E. Forster. The children too come again and again into view. We see him playing cards with them, taking them to the theatre, even exposing their quarrels. Further, too, there is quite plain in him a growing gentleness and sweetness, even in the midst of Prime Ministers and Rothschilds.

In 1865 he was appointed Assistant Commissioner on the Schools Inquiry Commission, which had to report upon Secondary Education in England and Wales. Arnold had to report upon Middle and Upper Class Education in France, Germany, Switzerland and Italy. This appointment gave him the opportunity for travel and nothing pleased him more. He saw Guizot, Sainte-Beuve, the Schérers. He went to Rome, Florence, and all the Italian University towns, and Berlin. Returning in the autumn of 1865 he was at work on the " Lectures on Celtic Literature," published in the *Cornhill*. By this time he had attracted the attention of England as seen by his visits to various homes. All the great names come into notice, Disraeli, Carlyle, Bright and Tennyson. He applied for Mr. Gladstone's recommendation of him to the post of Librarian to the House of Commons, but did not obtain the post. He had applied the year previously for a Commissionership under the Endowed Schools Act.

In 1866 he moved to West Humble, Dorking, the name of the place, as he wrote to Lady de Rothschild, perfectly suiting his nature. His letters at this time are full of references to the spreading influence of the Essays and Lectures as they appeared. And there are also those many reflections upon his increasing age, as if he had always the sense of the movement of time; revolt, too, against the social demands; attachment to solid and edifying reading such as Bishop Wilson's " Maxims," and so many lines a day of Greek; delightful vignettes of his children. And then, in 1868, the sudden descent of tragedy, first in the loss of Basil, on January 4th, and then on November 23rd, Tom, his eldest son, at the age of sixteen. The real character of a man is shown in these experiences, and the letters which refer to his loss are not only lovely for the fatherly heart which speaks in them, but they fix for us most truly the deep anchorage of Arnold's spirit. Little Basil was buried at Laleham; to be followed before the year was gone by his brother Tom.

In March the same year, he moved to Harrow. This year, 1868, seemed the beginning of an epoch for him. He refers to the gradual settlement of his thought, along with the death of his boys. And the reader will notice here, too, the interesting number of references to his father, to Biblical reading, and the deeper moral tone which sounds in his work. Mr. Geo. W. E. Russell, in editing the " Letters," wisely concludes the first volume in 1868, thus marking a distinct period in Arnold's life, exactly half-way between 1848 and 1888, the year of his death.

At the end of 1868 Arnold had established himself securely in English intellectual life. On the educational side he was bringing fresh ideas into the political world, freshly and forcibly expressed. On the literary side he was pouring out a stream of fine judgment upon men and books. On the social side he was publishing, month by month, in the *Cornhill*, the papers afterwards collected as " Culture and Anarchy," while at this time his poetry was widening this influence by its personal appeal.

Along with two other sterling individualities—
Carlyle and Ruskin—Arnold stood out in public
life in some respects the most arresting and certainly the most engaging of the three.

From 1868 on, Arnold took a more pronounced
and assertive attitude in English life. His experience on the Continent, his seventeen years in
provincial school-inspecting, his father's name, his
Oxford career, the originality and distinction of his
literary work, all gave that authority to his utterance
which enabled him to move out into a wider sweep
of criticism. For the next ten years, to about 1877,
we find him working in a new sphere of theology
and Biblical criticism. There came first " St. Paul
and Protestantism," " Literature and Dogma," and
" God and the Bible." The literary lovers do not
like Arnold in this realm. Prof. Saintsbury labels
the period " In the Wilderness," and drops over it
his witty acid. But it is Arnold, and in some sense
his most influential work. All this time he is
living a charming home life, going to Lord's with his
boys, fishing, skating, bathing, buying a pig,
botanising, meeting Huxley, Browning, Tennyson,
and Bagehot and bishops, and continuing his
friendly correspondence with Lady de Rothschild,
and doing a little speculation in stocks. In 1870, on
the suggestion of Lord Salisbury, he was made
Doctor of Civil Law at Oxford, Lord Bryce pre-
senting.

In 1871 he received the Order of Commander of the Crown of Italy, in recognition of his taking care of Prince Thomas of Savoy, in his household at Harrow. He was also invited to, but declined, the Middlesex Bench of Magistrates. All kinds of homely interests appear also: " Toss," the cat, has a long notice, and " Rover " must not be away from home on his birthday; he is shooting, " sport of the Barbarians," as he says, and missing badly; he is learning Hebrew; he again meets Lord Beaconsfield. Then the stroke of Fate falls and his son, Trevenen William Budge, died on February 16th, aged eighteen years, thus joining in death his two brothers.

In 1873 he left Harrow and took a house at Cobham called Pains Hill Cottage, where he lived until his death in 1888. During these fifteen years some of his most important work was done in this house, and the beautiful scenery of the district was a constant source of pleasure for him. Mrs. Ward has drawn a picture of his room, his writing-table, and the various personal details of a great man's surroundings. Soon after, his mother, aged eighty-two, dies. He stays to note in her character the remarkable way in which she appreciated his own work, although she had been trained to different convictions. What deep affection Matthew Arnold cherished for his mother is seen in the many and lovely letters that passed between them. More recently, Mrs. Humphry Ward, her granddaughter, has drawn a vivid picture of Mrs. Arnold, emphasizing the great fact of her life that she was left a widow with nine children—and such children. She was the centre of Fox How, and there is something noble and singular in the lives of the distinguished children who surrounded her. Up to her death, Matthew Arnold wrote to her regularly, keeping her closely informed on the reception which his writings were receiving. She certainly must have felt the shock of change in her son's ideas.

What would have been the correspondence between Matthew and Dr. Thomas Arnold? What would the latter have thought of passages in " Literature and Dogma " and " God and the Bible " ? Still his work presses on. The address to Westminster teachers, " A Speech at Westminster; " the fourth edition of " Literature and Dogma; " translations of part of Isaiah, of which he sent a copy to Cardinal Newman. The letter in reply to this was published in *The Times Literary Supplement*, in March, 1921, and another one from the Cardinal was supplied by Arnold's grandson, Mr. Arnold Whitridge. Then the reply to criticisms, " God and the Bible; " the two lectures on " Bishop Butler and the Zeit-Geist," bringing personal praise from Mr. Gladstone.

Incidentally, Arnold refers to his " many years

of isolated reflection and labour." And this is a note which it is well to mark, for the output of pure intellectual work in these years is remarkable. Every detail discloses new ideas, new expressions, and nothing appeared but what was worthy to be preserved, the School Inspector's work going on at the same time. Some years later, at the close of his lectures in America, he was entertained by the Authors' Club. He spoke in reply to their greeting and said that he " thought he owed this generous support to their finding in him that which pleased Gil Blas on the road to Merida, when he cried ' le cœur au métier '—the heart in the business. He believed that he had ' le cœur au métier.' " His sustained and varied work at this time is an excellent illustration. Mr. Gladstone stops him in the street, Disraeli greets him at the entrance to the Athenæum. In every direction is evidence of the immense working of his ideas. We have noted that the ten years, 1867-1877, were occupied principally with Biblical, theological and philosophical subjects, all treated in an unprofessional way, treated with an eye on Life itself, as Arnold would have said. Professor Saintsbury names this period " In the Wilderness," and then passes on to what he calls the " Last Decade," that is, 1878-1888. Certainly there is a division. The subject changes but the ideas come on anew. One after another, articles appeared in perfect manner, distinguished in tone and judgment

and rising higher and higher in level of style. There
came as single articles, first Mixed Essays and Irish
Essays, and the essays collected in the second
volume of " Essays in Criticism."

In 1880 he spent a holiday in Switzerland,
there meeting Mr. Mundella, his chief, and Henry
Labouchere. Apart from the steady output of
work, little happened in the next few years. In
1883 Mr. Gladstone conferred on him a pension
of £250 per annum, which he hesitated at first to
accept, but the excellent sense of business in him
asserted itself and we note shortly after that he began
his American tour, and this too brought him a fair
sum of money. This visit began in October
1883 and he returned in March 1884. He had
some difficulty at first in making himself heard, and
on the advice of his agent, Major Pond, took lessons
in elocution. Mrs. Arnold and his daughter
accompanied him. The lectures given were those
afterwards collected as American Discourses and
are well known typical expressions of the Arnold
personality. To bring a man of his judgment into
the American atmosphere was to invite light, and
there are many indications of a curious mixture
of appreciation for and hostility to that great civilisation. But he certainly enjoyed himself. His vitality
and zest for the new had ample scope in America.
He met Mr. Carnegie, Whittier, General Grant,
Wendell Holmes, Ward Beecher, the Vanderbilts,

the Astors.   It is curious how again and again he notes the absence of quiet, although universal enjoyment and good nature were present everywhere.

In 1885 he was again visiting Germany and met Mommsen, some of the German Court, and Dr. Döllinger.   In 1886 Mrs. Arnold went to New York to see her daughter Lucy, Mrs. Whitridge, and to become a grandmother.   Matthew Arnold followed on May 22nd.   " My Lucy's baby "—later called the Midget—"is a real pleasure to me, and I nurse it a great deal " he writes.   Indeed every human experience seemes to interest him.   His eye is open for scenery, climate and temperature, for plants, for trees and flowers.   But English Politics, then occupied with Gladstonian Home Rule, were constantly in his mind.   He stayed three days with Mr. Carnegie, and made his host stop by a stream that he might see the rhododendrons !   His critical mind is at work on America.

" Nothing in the book " (" Triumphant De-mocracy," by Mr. Carnegie) " touches the capital defect of life over here :   namely, that compared with life in England it is so uninteresting, so without savour and depth."   And we should note in the same letter (to Sir M. Grant-Duff), his botanical interest increasing as his years advanced. So also in the same letter we find reference to heart trouble.   And this frequently recurs.   A dangerous accident while bathing is mentioned and constant complaints of pains in the chest, which grow ominous. The letters of this time are full of life and insight. South Africa, he says in October 1886, should be watched. There is an exceedingly keen reference to General Grant as being " Selbständig," " broad and strong-sighted as well as firm charactered."

Upon his return from America he resigned his Inspectorship, April 30th 1886, and all the while botanical interests grow with his increased leisure. But many calls for literary contributions came to him. The articles on General Grant, on Tauler, on Amiel, on Sainte-Beuve, on the new education, on St. Paul and Protestantism all belong to this time. Still the political interest holds him. Mr. Goschen writes to him just before his succession to Lord Randolph Churchill. And he hires a fly to take his sister to see a field of cowslips, and finds a road where the nightingales sing continually.

Then came the famous article on Shelley, and one on Disestablishment, and an address on Milton at the unveiling of a window to him in St. Margaret's Church, Westminster, and an article on Tolstoi. Then we draw quickly to the end. His daughter, the wife of a New York lawyer, Mr. F. W. Whitridge, was expected home from America in early April, 1888.

The last published letters are full of references to the " Midget," his granddaughter. His father's heart was joyfully preparing to greet his daughter again. He went on the 14th April 1888, from Cobham to Liverpool expecting to meet Mrs. Whitridge on the following day. It is said that this night he was reading in bed the sixth volume of George Sand's Letters. In the morning, Sunday morning, he heard the Rev. John Watson, of Sefton Park, preach. While coming downstairs he was heard to be saying softly the first lines of the hymn, "When I survey the wondrous Cross," and at lunch he praised the hymn as the finest in the English language. In the afternoon he was out walking and, it is said, while jumping over low railings, suddenly died, at the age of 65 years and three months.

In appearance Arnold was tall, with jet black hair, a strong, rugged face, a large mouth, lined brow, a Jewish and Celtic type. His eyes were pleasant and humorous, and his urbane manner and free graceful carriage are frequently mentioned. It is said that he was exquisitely dressed, and of course the monocle worn is well known from his portraits. It is curious that his portraits all vary in expression. Watts's painting in the National Gallery suggests his spiritual nature, and that characteristic of natural mysticism which is so marked in his poetry, while several portraits suggest most clearly the Inspector. He is commemorated principally by a bust in Westminster Abbey, by a medallion in Rugby Chapel, and by a bust in the Passmore

Edwards College, Tavistock Square, and there is
a memorial window to him in St. Mary's Church,
Ambleside.

The principal events of his early life are, as we
have seen, found in connection with Dr. Arnold; the
principal official events of his life are associated with
his educational work ; the real light, however,
upon Arnold comes through Mr. Russell's edition
of his letters. This revealed a new, unknown
Arnold. Here was shown a devoted husband,
an affectionate father, and here was unfolded a
simple life of domestic joy and sorrow associated
unseen with a continuous production of infinitely
powerful thought. Rarely in English life has
there been such a review of the whole expanse
of a nation's life made from such a quiet station.
But could it have been better ? Arnold, of course,
by his name and by his genius commanded respect
in and had access to all English Society. The
friendship with the Rothschilds stands out. But
there was an unusual simplicity in his mode of
life, and none of that dangerous service to Society
which inflicts so often such loss upon the
giver.

By contrast a selection of Arnold's note-books
has been published, and this has given us a unique
acquaintance with his inner life. These note-books
are the witness to a culture of the spirit strangely
unlike the gay and free witticisms spent upon solemn

subjects. But no man ever so pruned his life ; and the result is seen in the judgment of every man who came into contact with Arnold. Beautiful testimony to this is on record in the words of Lord Coleridge and Mr. Geo. E. Russell.

From the latter we know that Arnold attended the services of the Church, even taking the Communion. And in this connection Mr. Russell has preserved several interesting personal records ; that Arnold liked to hear the Athanasian Creed sung, " 'But one God' sounds so magnificently, with that full swell of the organ. It seems to come with the whole authority of the Church " (" Matthew Arnold," p. 266) ; that he habitually used a Bible, a gift from his godfather, John Keble ; that in giving a prayer book to a child he wrote on the fly-leaf, "We have seen His Star in the East, and are come to worship Him."

Many stories of his school life have been kept. One schoolmaster describes him giving a dictation test. " It was about an adventure with wolves, and I recollect to this day his deep voice as he sauntered up and down in front of the class declaiming the phrase, ' the wolves howled,' and, for the sake of the young examinees, rolling out the word ' howled ' over and over again, with an unmistakable aspirate and final ' d.' " To one teacher he expresses his wish to see the roses on her cheeks when he visits the school again. To

Mr. Russell again we are indebted for a vivid portrait of Arnold in school-work :

" There must be many who still remember with amused affection his demeanour in an elementary school. They see the tall figure, at once graceful and stately ; the benign air, as of an affable arch-angel ; the critical brow and enquiring eye-glass bent on some very immature performance in pen-manship or needlework ; and the frightened children and the anxious teacher, gradually lapsing into smiles and peace, as the great man tested the proficiency in some such humble act as spelling. ' Well, my little man, and how do you spell dog ?' ' Please sir, d-o-g.' ' Capital, very good indeed, I couldn't do it better myself. And now let us go a little further, and see if we can spell cat.' (*Chorus excitedly*) ' C-a-t.' ' Now this is really excellent.' (*To the teacher*) ' You have brought them on wonderfully in spelling since I was here last. You shall have a capital report. Good-bye.' " (" Matthew Arnold," p. 98.)

The generation which knew Arnold personally is now quickly passing away. The charm of his society, and the individuality which added to his written word the power of a living recollection will disappear with those who were fortunate enough to meet him. But records are rich enough to capture and retain it for future generations. Above all, the delightful portraiture of his home life outlined by his letters has made Arnold widely known to those interested in the problems which occupied his mind.

What is above all necessary is to conceive Arnold in the midst of his generation preaching truths of criticism, truths of appeal acutely needed. As we recede from the Victorian era its disagreeable features are plain enough. Religion was presented in extremes of hideousness on one side in the form of Evangelicalism cruelly and insolently threatening hell fire to those not accepting its crude superstitions, and on the other side in Anglicanism ritual attracting the mental dotage of the age. Over against this came Arnold by individual voice raising the note of reason, undermining the fabric of impossibility and quietly speaking out an emancipated interpretation of Christianity. In another direction, wealth was pursued by the same people, regardless of human rights. This was the twofold pursuit of the Victorian era. " How to make the best of both worlds ! " as one of the Nonconformist leaders candidly phrased it. Pure Victorianism ! A generation being taught to pursue such a religion and such objects in life, what wonder that the rest of the Victorian civilisation should take its character from the central features ! Hypocrisy stalking in the Churches, putrid poverty, deep and shameful and unregarded, everywhere spread around. Politicians reciting party-airs, oblivious of the deeper needs of the nation. The nation itself among other European nations losing force and influence, and regarded as senile. Such in a few words was the spectacle of Victorian England. Individual men of genius were plentiful enough, but their greatness was magnified by the mediocrity of the many.

Later years have realised keenly the defects of the age, but it was given to Arnold, and with him we may place Ruskin and Carlyle, to see the faults from within. Hence the whole of Arnold's life-work must be regarded as a criticism of Victorianism ; its aristocracy, its middle-class, its lower class, its religion, its commercialism, its ugliness, its ignorance, its press, its taste, its pleasures, its leaders, its foreign policy, its industrialism, its whole fabric. Arnold's critical genius found ample scope. In turn every phase of social life was illuminated and condemned by him. He was effective by his personality. The gods with insight placed him completely endowed in the middle of the age which required him. Nothing could be more appropriate than that he, so finely equipped with gifts of intellectual analysis, and not less with the high sensitiveness of the artist, should be shot into a civilisation so devoid of them. Upon every spot he turned his arrows finely barbed round the whole circle from every direction to every place. The Victorian age produced its own critic and is for ever truly photographed in his pages.

POETRY

BIBLIOGRAPHY

1840. " Alaric at Rome."
1843. " Cromwell."
1849. " The Strayed Reveller," and other Poems.
1852. " Empedocles on Etna."
1853. Poems.
1855. Poems. (Second Series.)
1858. " Merope."
1867. New Poems.
1869. Poems. (1st Collected Edition.)
Later. Various editions of Collected Poems with a few additions.

THE first step is to relate Arnold's poetry to his life. One fact is all important. By the age of 33 he had produced the principal part of his poetry. It is true that between the age of 33 and 45 he added several pieces of the highest order, particularly several of his great Elegies. But from the age of 45 onwards, with the one exception of " Westminster Abbey," he wrote nothing of great importance. This then is the feature of his poetry ; it is a poetry of his youth. By 1855, that is when he was 33, he had completed the chief part of his

44

poetical work and by 1867 almost all. Why this cessation ? He had, so to speak, made his name, as we shall see later. His " Essays in Criticism," the Professorship at Oxford, the Education Commissions with which he worked, the Continental travels and, arising out of these, his social works beginning with " Culture and Anarchy," had established him prominently in the public mind. But these were all signs that the critical bent had mastered the poetical, and as the former asserted itself in him the poet became silent. So that Arnold's poetry is apart from the rest of his work ; it arouses no antipathies and appeals to minds who otherwise, perhaps, almost dislike him. It is an intensely personal and intimate poetry revealing his own mind. Here was its power for Arnold's generation, and when the environment of his mental life has disappeared it may be that much of his poetical influence will too have disappeared.

Arnold entered Oxford in the year in which Newman went over to Rome. The Tractarian movement was followed by a reaction in the direction of naturalistic and critical views. Arnold became the voice of that reaction. On every side old beliefs, old institutions, were being undermined, new scientific discoveries appeared to be destroying the foundations of the Christian faith, as it was then conceived, and doubt like a grey mist spread over the whole field of thought. But by inheritance

Arnold had a distinct influence. He had the sense of historic affection. He knew and prized the great Christian institution which science appeared likely to destroy. It is this acquiescence in the critical position in combination with his love for the Church which appealed to his admirers. This is the master key to his poetry. A poet has many sides. One reader will fix on one characteristic and single out the poems which illustrate it. Hence a Romanticist will select " Tristram and Iseult"; the Classicist will say " Merope ; " the Words-worthian will quote the " Youth of Man." But the dominant note—not necessarily the highest reach—the moving spirit of his work is found in " Ober-mann " and " Dover Beach " and stanzas from the " Grande Chartreuse " and " Rugby Chapel " with its noble eulogy, the eulogy of his father. Indeed the whole of the poems published before he was 45 contain that particular combination of the ethical and the critical elements which makes its special appeal to most of Arnold's followers. But specially is this true of " Rugby Chapel."

This poem might be chosen as most typical of Arnold. It is dignified and noble in diction, it is the very ideal of affection and reverence for a father and teacher, it is the voice of a deeply religious soul, its imagery is perfect and surpassingly appro-priate, it has lines of fragrant power for the spirit, clinging lines of melodious beauty and all through

a solemnity of tone, rising at the end to a pure
height of vision. There is most evident in it
that positive ideal of quiet, beneficent, clearly
directed work as the law of the individual life, which
was the guiding power of both father and son,
and the forming power upon others:

> " But thou would'st not *alone*
> Be saved, my father ! alone
> Conquer and come to thy goal,
> Leaving the rest in the wild.
> We were weary, and we
> Fearful, and we in our march
> Fain to drop down and to die.
> Still thou turnedst, and still
> Beckonedst the trembler, and still
> Gavest the weary thy hand.
>
> If, in the paths of the world,
> Stones might have wounded thy feet,
> Toil or dejection have tried
> Thy spirit, of that we saw
> Nothing—to us thou wast still
> Cheerful, and helpful, and firm !
> Therefore to thee it was given
> Many to save with thyself ;
> And, at the end of the day,
> O faithful shepherd ! to come,
> Bringing thy sheep in thy hand."

On the intellectual side, the critical side, he can
be seen best in the two Obermann poems. They
exhibit the destructive work of his generation.

He felt himself to be standing amid the ruins of old systems yet feeling too their practical value. Hence the poignant sense of loss. What Arnold felt appealed to many minds ; and it is just this intimate and personal identity of experience which is the secret of Arnold's possessive power over certain sections of our community. He had gone through the critical process, but he had in a measure saved his soul, and having done so saved others. In this light alone can Arnold be fully appreciated :

> " Now he is dead ! Far hence he lies
> In the lorn Syrian town ;
> And on his grave, with shining eyes,
> The Syrian stars look down."

Then he had a particular and distinct view of Nature, and this gives his poems a special value and appeal to some readers. It is not that of Wordsworth, who saw in Nature a vast, benevolent Power overshadowing mankind with wings of love ; nor Browning's view, who saw in Nature the woven threads of a plan progressing from ignoble origins to measureless grandeur. Nor was it simply descriptive poetry. What it is can be stated best by saying that he saw Nature as an assemblage of vast Powers set in their places, isolated, majestic, and unchanging, performing allotted duties with effortless calm ; thus being exemplars to man. Solitude, calm, eternal vastness,

these are the prevalent ideas. Then to these
he added, or better, he unified these by the sense
of personality with which he invested Nature.
To see this the whole poem, " The Youth of
Nature," should be read with its complementary
" Youth of Man," beginning :

> " We, O Nature, depart,
> Thou survivest us ! this,
> This, I know, is the law.
> Yes ! but more than this,
> Thou who seest us die
> Seest us change while we live ;
> Seest our dreams, one by one,
> Seest our errors depart ;
> Watchest us, Nature ! throughout,
> Mild and inscrutably calm."

By this binding quality of personality and the
separate ideas of the isolation, the vast remove, the
passionlessness of Nature, he produced a perfectly
individual doctrine of Nature, which moves his
readers, his disciples, with power. We refer
to the poems " Quiet Work," " In Harmony with
Nature," the exalted poem " In Utrumque Paratus,"
" Resignation," the Switzerland poems, " Lines
written in Kensington Gardens." We turn aside
for a moment to see the origin of this particular
Arnold view of Nature. It can be traced to
Goethe and to Wordsworth. In his article on
Spinoza (" Essays in Criticism," Vol. I), Arnold

D

states the view of Nature which Spinoza gave to Goethe. It is Arnold's own.

> " Spinoza first impresses Goethe and any man like Goethe, and then he composes him ; first he fills and satisfies his imagination by the width and grandeur of his view of Nature, and then he fortifies and stills his mobile, straining, passionate, poetic temperament by the moral lesson he draws from his view of Nature. And a moral lesson not of mere resigned acquiescence, not of melancholy, quietism, but of joyful activity within the limits of man's true sphere."

Let us repeat some of this ; composes him, fills and satisfies his imagination, fortifies and stills; not acquiescence but joyful activity. No words could better express the Arnold conception, the Arnold use of Nature. Spinoza to Goethe, Goethe to Arnold is the succession. The overshadowing influence of Wordsworth is natural. Fox How, the home of his childhood, Wordsworth's friendship with the family and the poetic setting of the district account sufficiently for the cast of his poetry.

We should notice here Arnold's gift of graphic description. By night or by day there is the same lucid drawing of perfectly clear outlines and an exquisite power of producing a very photograph of some natural scene, some vision of cloud or mountain or vale, or in detail some minute cameos of a natural scene.

" When garden walks and all the grassy floor
  With blossoms red and white of fallen May,
  And chestnut-flowers are strewn."

" Soon will the high Midsummer pomps come on,
  Soon will the musk carnations break and swell,
  Soon shall we have gold-dusted snapdragon,
  Sweet-William with his homely cottage smell
  And stocks in fragrant blow !
  Roses that down the alleys shine afar,
  And open, jasmine-muffled lattices,
  And groups under the dreaming garden-trees,
  And the full moon, and the white evening star."

The personal religious history of Arnold's mind
and his view of Nature supply the main elements of
his poetry. They are intellectual elements and
give the character to it. Arnold is not pessimistic.
His sentiment is rather a sentiment of the mind
than of the feelings. For this reason probably he
will never be a popular poet.

He took a wide range in selecting his subjects,
Egypt, Greece, Persia and the Mediæval world.
His manner is classical. He chose classical forms
as in " Merope," and made imitations of Greek
types. Both of his two long dramatic poems are
Greek in form. Of these " Merope " is the
dullest of all his work and " Empedocles " has
scarcely a dramatic touch at all.

But there are characteristics in his poetry which
are distinctly classical. Simplicity, lucidity, restraint,
dignity, pathos, all these are peculiarly and superbly

qualities of his poetry.   In a marked way he showed balance, measure, self-control.   There are no eccentricities, no violences, no extravagances of any kind.   Restraint, equableness, these are the tones of his work and these attach him to the classics. One cannot compare his accomplishments with the sublimer strokes of Swinburne, but he has what Swinburne lacks, a poignant sense of humanity ; " Balder Dead " in subject is Scandinavian, " Sohrab and Rustum " is Persian, but in manner they are Greek. The severity, the direct, exact and simple statement, an atmosphere of pure light and an almost complete absence of colour, avoidance of adjectives, all these are Arnold's and are signs of the classical influence.

> " Back ! with the conscious thrill of shame
> Which Luna felt, that summer night,
> Flash through her full immortal frame,
> When she forsook the starry night
> To hang over Endymion's sleep
> Upon the pine-grown Latmian steep."

> " I see the night dews,
> Cluster'd in thick beads, dim
> The agate brooch-stones
> On thy white shoulder :
> The cool night-wind, too,
> Blows through the portico,
> Stirs thy hair, Goddess,
> Waves thy white robe ! "

Above all there is in Arnold's poetry that quality of pathos which gives it a Vergilian character. At one time personal as in " Tristram and Iseult," or " Balder Dead," or " Sohrab and Rustum," at another intellectual as in " Obermann," or sentimental as in the " Faded Leaves " poems, it is always present; poignant or majestic, it is all through Arnold's work, and it is to a certain extent the note of Greek and of Latin. In some sense it might be said that pathos is the most conspicuous of the Arnold traits. If one takes a quick general view of the whole of his poetry, pathos can be seen as a strain running though it all. The weird legend of " The Forsaken Merman," the anguish of a father in " Sohrab and Rustum," the tragic beauty of " Tristram and Iseult," the heavier gloom of " Merope," the last victorious grief of " Empedocles," all are united by this keen perception of unpitying Fate which overtakes the individual. Moreover there is the same pathos only raised to the world of thought in many other poems. What is " Obermann " but a spirit's tragedy ? " The Scholar Gypsy," the " Grande Chartreuse " have each this same character of grief, only grief of the spirit. Present in all his work is Arnold's sense of individual isolation in life.

But in order to define the limits of the classical influence we must note the great part which Nature takes in creating his poetical work, and by this he is completely separated from the classical character. This fills his poems with a modern appeal, gives him the vital modern tone; classicism is simply in Arnold the vesture of his writing.

The foregoing are the principal characteristics of his poetical work. We might treat it by what it lacks. The qualities of his poetry are so distinct that one can see rapidly how Arnold differs from other poets. The intellectual character of his work almost compels the absence of emotion. The austere view of life, the constant emphasis upon the fact of man's aloofness in nature, and upon the need of control, imply the absence of passion, emotion, exaltation. Where these are present they have a kind of intellectual transmutation which deprives them of their true quality. It is, after all, not passion, not emotion, not exaltation, but thought, perception, reflection. Meredith's utter and personal casting of his soul before the reader, Swinburne's intimate declarations of passion, Rossetti's spiritual exaltation, these are unknown in Arnold.

His poetry appeals specially to those who by time and training have felt the dissolvent force of historical and literary criticism upon religious institutions ; it attracts those who by temperament are lovers of nature with the philosophical mind. It engages every mind which appreciates English utterance without obscurity, without superfluity, utterance through the fine word, the noble word, utterance of the pathos of fact and the still deeper utterance of intellectual grief. With these general remarks upon Arnold's poetry there are some observations worth the making.

Of these first it is noticeable that Arnold's satire rarely, possibly only once, entered his poetry. Curious also is it that his editors and appreciators all differ in their selections of his best. " Sohrab and Rustum" " Thyrsis " " The Strayed Reveller " " The Scholar Gypsy " "A Summer Night " " The New Sirens " each has been chosen but each reader seems to find his best in a separate choice. A still more curious thing is that the one piece of Arnold which may be called a failure, " Merope," was produced by a theatrical company some years ago in East London. We give the newspaper note as an interesting fact which may stimulate the imagination :

"Matthew Arnold's ' Merope ' will be presented by the People's Free Theatre Company on Saturday next, at 8 o'clock, at the Passmore Edwards Settlement, and during February and March there will be nine performances of the play at Leytonstone, the Borough, Walthamstow, Toynbee Hall, Canning Town, Whitechapel, and Bethnal Green."

At the last the question of comparison will arise. Was he of the greatest ? Arnold himself was firm in the placing of the great names. Where shall we place him? That he had visitations of the Holy Spirit of Poetry is beyond question. Line after line bears the accent and witness of the Divine. The very breath and motion of supreme genius lives in passage after passage. That peculiar vision, that touched utterance, that ascent to the Universal is unmistakable in him—" Murmurs and scents of the infinite sea." But yet he is only the master of a minority. His very personal environment and his mental history set him down for the few, but for that few he is supreme, and for them the master voice. Arnold produced work of such recognised power in such different spheres of life that it is difficult to select any one part which stands out supreme above the rest. Yet as to creative work, that precious individual element which constitutes the soul of genius, his poetry supplies perhaps the principal claim. By that he is high indeed in the rich ranks of English poets.

Yet this beautiful, immortal work, of finished beauty and most intimate and instant appeal to the Victorian age, came unheeded. His first volume, published in his 27th year in 1849, " The Strayed Reveller and other Poems" by A. London (B. Fellowes, Ludgate Street, 1849, 500 copies, price 4s. 6d.), was withdrawn from circulation before many copies were sold. William Rossetti, then under 20, reviewed it favourably ; the *Blackwood* abused it. His second volume, "Empedocles on Etna" 1852, was withdrawn before 50 copies were sold. He withdrew them apparently for the reason which was stated in a letter to the Rev. Herbert Hill, a tutor in the Arnold family, dated November 5, 1852, a month after publication of the book.

> "The strain of thought generally is no doubt much too doleful and monotonous. I had no notion how monotonous till I had the volume printed before me. I thought, too, when the poems were in manuscript, that they would possess a more general attraction than their predecessors; I now see that they will not—and on this head I am sure you are quite right—and it is a great fault; no one will more readily allow this than I. But I hope still to do better some day."

So the Rev. Herbert Hill advised him badly. The same letter contains Arnold's account of the origin of "Tristram and Iseult." This letter, like the Newman letters, first found its way to the *Times Literary Supplement*.

The poetic light in it was seen, for when Arnold later in 1867 reprinted "Empedocles" he stated that he did so at the request of "a man of genius, whom he had the honour and the good fortune to interest, Mr. Robert Browning." We said his first volume, "The Strayed Reveller" was published in 1849. Before that date the prize poem "Alaric" was printed at Rugby in 1840, and the

Newdigate Prize Poem, " Cromwell " was printed at Oxford in 1843, Arnold receiving £10 for the copyright. A third appearance is interesting. In *The Examiner*, 21st July, 1849, he published anonymously a Sonnet, " To the Hungarian Nation." It was not republished, as Arnold did not think much of it. We should notice in it the echo of the 1848 spirit. Then came the " Strayed Reveller," 1849, and " Empedocles," 1852. In 1853 came the volume of collected and new poems under Arnold's own name, and so on in fairly fast succession, second edition 1854, then a second series, 1855. By this time his reputation was firmly established. Once more we turn back to " The Strayed Reveller," 1849, to survey his living contemporaries. Wordsworth was alive, and Laureate, Tennyson had established a reputation, Browning was rising, yet each of these was coldly received. Prof. Saintsbury (" Matthew Arnold," p. 10) describes the period as one of the nadir of English criticism, and refers to its neglect of Thackeray, Tennyson, Carlyle, Ruskin, Borrow, FitzGerald, Browning. G. H. Lewis was editing *The Leader. The Westminster Review*, *The Examiner* and *The Critic* were all in the hands of distinguished men. But the " Strayed Reveller " volume went unheeded.

The interesting fact came to light in his published letters that he had worked for long upon a poem

on " Lucretius," and then abandoned it. One
verse apparently was published, prefixed to the first
editions of " Thyrsis."

> " Thus yesterday, to-day, to-morrow come,
> They hustle one another and they pass :
> But all our hustling morrows only make
> The smooth to-day of God."

EDUCATION

BIBLIOGRAPHY

1861.   " The Popular Education of France," with Notices of that of Holland and Switzerland.

1862.   " The Twice-Revised Code," *Fraser's Magazine*, March.

1863-1864.   " A French Eton, or Middle-Class Education and the State." *Macmillan's Magazine*, September, 1863, February, 1864, May, 1864.

1868.   " Schools and Universities on the Continent."

1874.   " Higher Schools and Universities in Germany." (The German portion of the 1868 volume.)

1874.   " A Speech at Westminster," *Macmillan's Magazine*, February.

1878.   " Irish Catholicism and British Liberalism," *Fortnightly Review*, July.

   " Porro Unum est Necessarium," *Fortnightly Review*, November.

1881.   " An Unregarded Irish Grievance."

1886.   " Special Report on Elementary Education on the Continent " (a Government Report afterwards issued as a pamphlet).

1887.   " Schools " (in the Reign of Queen Victoria. Edited by T. H. Ward, M.A.)

1889.   " Reports on Elementary Schools " (1852-1882).

Arnold's writings on education are divided into :

    I.   His Reports as an Inspector in Elementary Schools.

    II. His Reports on three educational Commissions.

    III. Miscellaneous articles, chiefly on Secondary Education.

I. (*a*) This past part of Arnold's work has been fully and authoritatively treated by Sir Joshua Fitch in his book on " Thomas and Matthew Arnold and their influence on English education."

Sir Joshua Fitch having been a colleague of Matthew Arnold's for many years and thus brought into close contact with him in the somewhat unattractive sphere of school inspection, his book is interesting as showing the praise which Arnold's daily work received from those who saw it near at hand. Mr. Thomas Healing, an assistant of Arnold's, contributes to Sir Joshua Fitch's book an article from the *Methodist Times*, describing Arnold's work from his personal standpoint. In 1851 Arnold was appointed Inspector of Schools by Lord Lansdowne, to whom he had been private secretary since 1847. He continued to occupy the post until his retirement in 1886; having thus rendered 35 years of public service. From the 14th April, 1851, until the 1st May, 1871, that is, until a New Code following the Elementary Educa-

tion Act, 1870, came into force, Arnold inspected
certain Elementary Schools in a large district, the
Midlands and Wales, covering about one third
of England and comprising about 4,000 schools,
with a Staff of about twenty Inspectors. At that
time only clergymen could inspect the schools
of the Church of England, and only Roman Catholics the schools of the Roman Catholic Church.
Arnold was thus limited to the schools of the
British and Foreign School Society, and to Wesleyan
and other Protestant Schools not connected with the
Church of England. This should be noted in
view of his later, severely critical attitude to Dissent.
By instructions, October 14, 1870, he became a
Chief Inspector in the Metropolitan Division of
Westminster and three outlying census divisions.
Denominational inspection was abolished, and he
had to visit all schools receiving public grants.
He had too the supervision of Inspectors in that
division. He occupied this post until he resigned
on the 30th April, 1886.

His letters are convincing evidence that he did
not like the work. He accepted the post in the
first place because its assured income enabled him
to marry. He forced his will to the work, but
disliked the routine, the detail and the mass of work
which took him away from more congenial literary
interests. Sir Joshua Fitch rightly points out that
the variety and freedom of his life as an inspector,

and the opportunity of arranging his own time were extremely valuable to Arnold. It is clear that his colleagues and those with whom he was brought into contact regarded him as being too good for the work. The official view of him is of course now inaccessible, but the opinion of his colleagues is represented in the following :

> " From the official point of view, he was not, it must be owned, an exacting Inspector. If he saw little children looking good and happy, and under the care of a kindly and sympathetic teacher, he would give a favourable report, without inquiring too curiously into the percentage of scholars who could pass the ' standard ' examination."—(" Thomas and Matthew Arnold," by Sir Joshua Fitch.)

The following also and the passage from Mr. Healing give authoritative judgment upon Arnold's work in this sphere :

> " But it is also true that his influence on schools was in its own way far more real and telling than he himself supposed. Indirectly, his fine taste, his gracious and kindly manner, his honest and generous recognition of any new form of excellence which he observed all tended to raise the aims and the tone of the teachers with whom he came in contact, and to encourage them in self-respect and respect for their work."—(" Thomas and Matthew Arnold," by Sir Joshua Fitch.)

> " He inspired many a young teacher with the desire to work in the direction of obtaining a London degree,

and even those who did not succeed were permanently benefited by the efforts they made. If he found a young man of promise in a school, he generally had with him some serious and sympathetic talk on this subject, and some have told me in the after years that they would never have attempted a work of such difficulty but for the stimulus applied by Mr. Arnold."—(Mr. Thomas Healing, quoted in "Thomas and Matthew Arnold," by Sir Joshua Fitch.)

"His usefulness as an Inspector appears to me very much in his success in bringing some tincture of letters into the curriculum of the Elementary School."—*Ibid*.

(*b*) His inspectorial Reports have had the distinction of republication, and contain much valuable observation and suggestion upon Elementary Teaching. They cover the long period 1852-1882; and the extracts from Reports on Training Colleges cover the period 1853-1868. These were collected and edited by Sir Francis Sandford, afterwards Lord Sandford, and published soon after Arnold's death, and have since been republished by the Board of Education, and again for the Board of Education, with new additions, by Mr. F. S. Marvin in 1908. They show us the subjects which were occupying him in his daily toil for 35 years ; and remind us how closely connected were the interests of his leisure and the duties of his profession. His inspectorial work indeed supplied a solid basis for his social and political views. Behind the immediate Report we see the thinker interested in questions of national character ; and in education as it affected social characteristics. Passing over the great number of points of detail which necessarily belong to Annual Reports of this kind we fix on the following as specially noteworthy.

1. The frequent emphasis upon the cultivating of the intelligence as the chief end in the education of children ; and in literature the formation of taste by chosen pieces of the English classics.
2. Criticism of current school reading-books, for not containing the best and most suitable of English pieces.
3. Recommendation of the Bible—the main outlines and selected passages to be learned by heart—as being closely attached to the national life, and the source of the best English.
4. Recommendation of the practice of learning and reciting choice pieces of poetry ; re-commendation of Parsing and Analysis ; Geography, and Natural Science, and specially we should notice his recommendation of the teaching of universal History. On the other hand he disapproved of Physiology and Botany for elementary standards.
5. Criticism of the system of Payment by Results

introduced by the Revised Code, 1862, and the disarrangement of Pupil Teachers that followed ; and of the new method of examination by which the individual scholar in each standard was examined instead of the collective examination of a class in its spirit and cultivation as a whole.

(c) The Training Colleges inspected were the Westminster Wesleyan Training College, those of the British and Foreign Bible Society, and the Congregational College at Homerton. In 1870 the inspection of these Colleges became the work of special inspectors. The extract edited by Sir Francis Sandford extended from 1833-1868. On these he says :

> " His (Arnold's) report of this class, as a rule, dealt merely with the life and history of individual colleges for a single year, and would have no general interest. They are therefore not republished. But some extracts from them are retained, which relate to matters of principle, or appear for other reasons to be worthy of preservation."—(Introduction, page 7.)

There is special interest in these Reports as they give us further and, we think, little known information on the subject of Arnold's attitude towards Dissenters. His appreciation of the Wesleyan College at Westminster, and especially of the Wesleyan infant school system is clearly although cautiously expressed. His entire and emphatic approval of the Congregational system may be seen from the following :

" Still in seizing this notion of Evangelical Protestantism (as founded on the Bible and not, as in Catholicism, upon authority) as the basis of the religious character of their schools, and in guarding this, so far as they could, from being a mere unreal colourless thing, made up of vague generalities, the Congregational Board have had the merit of conceiving a type of popular school better suited, probably, to be the public school of the bulk of the people of this country than either the so-called National School or the Wesleyan School on the one hand, or than the British School, or still more, than the secular School, on the other ; and their conception has in it, in my opinion, elements of utility which may well bear fruit in the future."—(" Reports of Elementary Schools," page 291.)

Of various points referred to in the Reports we may note the interesting judgment as to the value of Music and Natural Science in comparison with Literature, and the recommendation of Univeral History as a subject for pupil teachers :

" . . . how musical and physical science seem each of them to awaken young men of the class to which these students belong (pupil-teachers) ; to be capable of striking the ' electric chain ' in them, in a way in which no other part of their instruction can. No doubt it is because of this capacity that the civilising power of music has always been famed so highly ; for instruction civilises a new nature only so far as it delights and enkindles it. Perhaps it will be found that physical science has, for such natures, something of a similar power, and that we may well make more use of both agents than we do at present. Undoubtedly no refining influence is more powerful than that of literary culture ; but this influence seems to need in the recipient a certain refinement of nature at the outset in order to make itself felt ; and with this previous refinement music and physical science appear able to dispense."—(" Reports on Elementary Schools," page 278.)

The last of these Reports contains a strong advocacy of the Bible as worthy of a large place in the primary education of children, notably on the ground of its poetry and philosophy; and a plea for the Catechism as a child's introduction to metaphysics. Finally there is an elucidation of the true use of the term " Evangelical " as identical with " Protestant," and not with the narrower application of it to a particular scheme of doctrine extracted from the New Testament.

The relations of an Inspector are delicate ; on the one hand with his superiors and on the other with the teachers. But Arnold's fine sense and clear perception were exactly in place here. He has set out admirably in the Report for 1854 the duties of an Inspector. The Revised Code of 1862 changed the method of inspection and lowered it, as Arnold thought, and as with perfect candour he said :

" The whole school felt under the old system that the prime aim and object of the Inspector's visit was, after ensuring the fulfilment of certain sanitary and disciplinary conditions, to test and quicken the intellectual life of the school. The scholars' thoughts were directed to this object, the teachers' thoughts were directed to it, the Inspector's thoughts were directed to it. . . . The new examination is in itself a less exhausting business than the old inspection to the person conducting it, and it does not make a call as that did upon his spirit and inventiveness, but it takes up much more time, it throws upon him a mass of minute detail, and severely tasks hand and eye to avoid mistakes."—(" Reports on Elementary Schools," pages 101 and 102.)

One feels that Arnold's abilities deserved some higher occupation than that of inspecting primary schools : yet, on the other hand, primary education gained. What Mr. Healing says, that Arnold brought some " tincture of letters " into the elementary schools, is true. While utilitarian views of the barrenest type were dominating the political side of popular education, it was a good thing for English life that Arnold at the spring of the educational waters was a stream of culture. Since Arnold's time Elementary Education —Primary Education as it is now called—has seen immense expansion, changes and disappearances. The names and institutions, programmes of Arnold's day have gone. Payment by results has gone. The Board of Education has been set up ; and Municipal authorities are linked with the Central authority in control. Kindergartens, physical training, medical inspection have been added.

The Reports described above laid down the principles which have regulated our Primary Education ; and every authority on Education—Fitch, Sadler, Marvin—has confirmed the effect of Arnold's work.

II. Our second division covers his work as Assistant Commissioner on two Education Commissions and a Special Inquiry for the Education Department.

1. The Commission to inquire into the state of Popular Education in England, appointed in 1858, with the Duke of Newcastle as Chairman.
2. The Commission to report on Secondary Education in England and Wales, appointed in 1865, with Lord Taunton as Chairman.
3. An appointment in 1885, to inquire upon four specific points of education in Germany, Switzerland and France.

The Reports of the first and second were published in 1861 and 1868 respectively in Blue Books and afterward reprinted in separate volumes. The third Report was published as a Parliamentary paper in 1886. It will be observed that the first and third

were Reports on Primary and the second on Secondary Education.

(1) The object of the Commission of 1858
was to ascertain the state of popular instruction
as regulated by the Minutes of 1845. The inquiry
was extended to France, Germany and the French
cantons of Switzerland. Arnold was appointed
for the French-speaking countries, Mark Pattison
for Germany. Arnold apparently was glad to get
free of his routine work, but said that he had no
special interest in popular education. (See
" Letters," Volume I, page 78.) While on this
mission he saw Guizot, Madame de Staël, Lacordaire, Prosper Mérimée, and Sainte-Beuve. It
was on this tour that he collected the materials
for his first published prose, " England and the
Italian Question," 1859.

It is interesting to notice, too, as an instance of
Arnold's extreme versatility, that we find him
directly after his return from the Parisian salons
and their littérateurs drilling twice a week in the
Queen's Westminster Rifle Volunteers. In connection with the Report the following extract
from a letter is interesting :

" . . . I am very busy now with my Report ; that is
because I was not busy with it when I ought to have
been, you will say ; but I was really not ready to write
when I was at Fox How, and should even be glad to let
the thing lie in my head a month or two more before I

write it. I have not even yet composed more than a sentence or two here and there of the Report as it will actually appear, though I have covered a good many sheets with notes and extracts. I have passed the last week at the British Museum, and to-day I receive from France a number of documents which I ought to have received months ago, and which would have saved me a world of trouble by coming sooner."—(Letter to Miss Arnold, Jan. 20th, 1860. "Letters," Volume I, page 113.)

The Report was published in 1861. It contains characteristic work of Arnold's : prose direct and lucid, the prose of a man with practical business in hand. There are the usual happy phrases and quotations, Guizot's, for example, " C'est le grandeur de notre pays que les ésprits ont besoin d'être satisfaits, en même temps que les interêts." There is, moreover, a view of things beyond the immediate scope of the Commission. Nothing suited Arnold better than to treat education in relation to the culture of a people. The large range of observation, therefore, raises the Report to the level of a political treatise. For in this treatment of the educational problem he applied freely and consistently his conception of the function and aim of the State. With this large view expressed in the most spirited prose we may safely commend these Reports to the readers of Arnold who otherwise avoid Blue Books.

The Report deals with Elementary Education

in France, Switzerland and Holland. France occupies the chief place, with 107 pages out of 146. Arnold first gives a history of primary instruction in France up to the Revolution, during the period after the Revolution up to 1833, the establishment of the present system in its main features by the law of 1833 and the later regulations of 1850, 1852 and 1854, then the " material result in money raised, schools founded, scholars under instruction; the moral result, in the quality of the instruction, the proficiency of the scholars, the effect, so far as can be ascertained, on the nation." In the course of the Report, Arnold severely criticises the lack in England of provision for middle-class education, and the current inspectorial system. He praises the French law, which he says is an influence for reason and equity. We shall see later that the idea of the " State " as representing the nation's best self is the motive power of Arnold's educational politics. Hence the frequent comparisons in the Report between France on the one side and England on the other where individual action is so good and collective action so bad :

" The high Roman and Imperial theory as to the duties and powers of the State has never obtained in England. It would be vain to seek to introduce it ; but it is also vain to waste time in decrying it. I believe, as every Englishman believes, that our Government is pernicious and dangerous, that the State cannot safely be trusted to undertake everything, to superintend everywhere. But I hope that I may be allowed, having made this profession of faith, to point out as may be necessary, without perpetually repeating it, some inconveniences of under-government; to call their attention to certain important particulars, in which, within the domain of a single great question, that of public education, the direct action of the State has produced salutary and enviable results."—(Page 19.)

We see here the germination of Arnold's *Etatisme* action by the State. Let us remember that he is writing in 1860 in the very zenith of *laissez-faire*, years before the Fabian Society, ten years before 1870, which A. V. Dicey marked as the commencement of the period of State action in England. Arnold was really one of the channels of influence between the Continent and England.

The Report describes the foundation of a lay and national system of education by the Revolution. It praises the English pupil-teacher system on the important question of religion. Arnold shows that the State does not make itself denominational, but recognises three, the three most important, religious bodies, Protestants, Roman Catholics and Jews. The conclusion of the French Report is wholly devoted to the inculcation of the duty of the Government, as that of the national reason to stimulate and illuminate the national intelligence.

He shows that France has a national system of education unpretending and of a low standard of instruction, but yet a beginning and a basis.

The actual working of the schools in Switzerland Arnold did not see, as he was there in holiday time. He describes their system as Christian, democratic, compulsory and gratuitous. He lays his finger upon a disquieting tendency of democracy in Switzerland, the tendency to the elimination of superiorities.

For the schools of Holland he is full of praise. " I have seen no primary schools worthy to be matched, even now, with those of Holland." An account is given of the founding of Dutch primary schools in 1784. Arnold emphasizes the high esteem in which public service is held; the care as to teachers' qualifications, their high salaries, and the general diffusion of education. The Dutch system of retaining elder scholars was the root of our own pupil-teachers institution. There is an excellent account of the true relations between Church and State on page 148. There is a strong sentence critical of the Dutch character : " Although very far assuredly from the weakness of decrepitude, its genius moves with the mechanic and inelastic march of a spirit whose prime is over." The closing paragraphs of the Report are magnificent prose. There is in them the perfect, stately manner and the rich political wisdom of Burke. Did we desire to fix upon the ideal union of thought and style we could not choose better than that paragraph (p. 156) of the Report which concludes with the question, " If then the State disbelieves in reason, when will reason reach the mob ? "

The statistics and descriptions in these Reports are now largely historical. On one point, however, they are interesting. At the time of Arnold's visit, the French system of concurrent denominational support had not been long enough tried for its results to be seen. We now know that it did not succeed. It was displaced by a purely secular system. In the second place it is important to observe, as we have already pointed out, that these Reports show us Arnold shaping and illustrating his chief political doctrine: the State acting in its collective capacity as the organ of the national reason.

In November of the same year, 1861, Arnold began an article afterwards published in *Fraser's Magazine*, of March 1862, with the title, " The Twice Revised Code." The circumstances under which this article was written were as follows: The Commission on Popular Education in England issued its Report in 1861. Two points connected with this concern us here. The first as to the efficiency of the teaching, the second as to grants. As to the first, the efficiency of the teaching, the facts are summarised in the following:

" Even in the best schools three out of every four children left before reaching the highest class, and therefore with only such a pretence of knowledge as was to be gained in the lower classes. They got little more than a trick of mechanically pronouncing the letters, and the words which they read conveyed hardly any ideas to their minds. They left school, they went to work, and in the course of a year they knew nothing at all. The schools were educating one in eight of the class of children for which they were intended."—(" English National Education." H. Holman, M.A. p. 152.)

But Arnold, who knew elementary schools well at this time and could compare them with foreign schools, thought that too much was made of this. As to the second, the question of grants, the Commission proposed to make two grants, one from general taxation to be given on the general efficiency of the schools, and one from the county rate to be given on attendance and passing of an examination; these to be proportionately two-fifths and three-fifths of the whole amount. But Mr. Lowe (afterwards Lord Sherbrooke), Vice-President of the Education Department in 1861, immediately went beyond these suggestions. He proposed among other alterations that the whole of the grant should be made dependent upon the examination. Thereupon arose a controversy ; so great was the opposition to the new proposals that the Revised Code had to be considerably amended. Finally the grant was to be given two-thirds on examination and one-third on attendance. Arnold indeed wanted to strike out the examination grant entirely. (" Letters," Volume I, page 170.)

The article before us was one of the chief influences in securing this alteration. Arnold realised the importance of the case. He described it as " the heaviest blow dealt at civilisation and social improvement in any time." (" Letters," Volume I, page 160.)

Sir James Shuttleworth sent a reprint of the article to every member of Parliament. The curious thing is that Arnold was in some anticipation, certainly not fear, of being dismissed by the officials of the Education Department.

The article is not in Arnold's usual style. It exhibits a quality not at all characteristic of him— a close grappling with the details of a subject in a serious, almost earnest, manner. What he writes usually is apparently spontaneous and labourless. Here, however, are elaborate, tabulated arguments. This is due perhaps to the fact that he was dealing with his professional subject, and felt its immediate personal interest; as for example, when Mr. Lowe criticized the inspectors. Much of the article is technical and the interest of some of it has passed.

Arnold's first point is that the Revised Code was intended to be an extension of education, but, as a matter of fact, by reducing the grant, tended to narrow it. The second point is that the Code is a prize-scheme, that is, the grant is to be made upon proficiency in the three R's.   He then deals with the reasons that were asserted to be the basis of the new Code.   The Commissioners had declared that seven-twentieths of the scholars were not properly trained in the three R's.   Arnold's reply is that school officials say that this is due to the shortness of school life.   He himself attributed this inefficiency to the lack of general intellectual cultivation in the home life of the scholars.   Improve this, he says, and the education of the children will improve.   He then attacks the "prize-scheme:"   the system of payment by results which would necessitate an immense system of individual examination.   The new proposals, he said, would make the inspectors simply an army of registering clerks.   He suggests that the number of State inspectors should be diminished and use made of the ordinary local diocesan inspectors; that the crowded list of subjects should be cut down; and the power of partial, if not entire, stoppage given to the inspectors.

The general attack here made upon the Code is that the Council ought not to have given way to the enemies of the school system, but quietly to have waited and changed the system prudently.   The passage about the general intellectual culture of the family as forming the real basis for the child's training shows how continuously Arnold's thoughts

were directed to social conditions as determining
the national character. This he put concisely in a
letter (Volume I, " Letters," page 162) : " ... The
State has an interest in the primary school as a
civilising agent, even prior to its interest in it as an
instructing agent." Arnold died before the re-
moval of the system of payment by results in
1897, but his views were completely justified by
events.

In 1863 Arnold was writing continuously.
In September the first part of a series of three
articles entitled " A French Eton " appeared: the
second in February, 1864, the third in May
1864. These articles were reprinted in 1864 as a
book entitled " A French Eton; " and this again
was reprinted in 1892 with that part of his 1868
Commission Report which deals with French
secondary schools. The materials for " A French
Eton " were collected while he was on the 1859
Commission. He was then reporting on Primary
Education, but had opportunities of seeing several
French secondary schools. Hence these articles
in which he began the greatest of his education
endeavours. There is evidence in his " Letters "
that he took great care with this writing.

" A French Eton " describes two typical French
secondary schools, the public Lyceum of Toulouse
(note, a French Lyceum is an educational institution
provided and maintained by the State, with aid

from the department and commune), and the
private school of Sorèze. In the former Arnold
notes especially the scientific training in the mother-
tongue, a training which English schools then did
not give; and the care with which the meals were set
out, contrasting with what Arnold remembered
of his own school days. In his account of Sorèze
the interesting thing is the sketch of its principal,
the famous Lacordaire. This description of two
typical French schools was the " point de départ "
for a powerful advocacy of the establishment in
England of a public system of secondary instruction.
Arnold makes a survey of the three great English
classes and their ideals. Private secondary education in England there was. For the aristocracy
there were the nine great public schools offering
cheap and efficient instruction, but not having the
securities of supervision and publicity. The cost
of the public school education was too great for the
middle-class, and of private schools there was not
sufficient provision. The remedy is with the
State.

Universities are founded and supported by the
State. Why not secondary schools ? The Oxford
and Cambridge Local Examinations are endeavours
to supply the need, but they are only dealt with a few
scholars of each school and these the best, leaving
untouched the general condition of the school.
Arnold proposed :

F

1. That £20,000 should be devoted to Secondary
   Education.
2. That a centre of Secondary Education should
   be set up in each county, the funds to come
   from—

       (*a*) Fees.
       (*b*) Endowments—some already existing.
       (*c*) Scholarships.

Arnold said that the cry would be raised : " The
State had better leave things alone." This arose
from a misconception of the State. " The State,"
as Burke said, " is a partnership of all its members
for common ends." A citizen, therefore, is not
humiliated by receiving education at its hands, any
more than the aristocracy is humiliated by using the
Universities with their endowments. The causes
making against the operation of the State in England
are :

1. The Aristocracy does not care to be over-
   shadowed.
2. The Middle-class dislikes it because—

       (*a*) The State in alliance with the High
       Church was the Middle-class oppressor.
       (*b*) Whereas the Aristocracy and the work-
       ing-class both have ideals, the Middle-
       class is self-satisfied.
       (*c*) It knows that the State manages things
       badly.

Arnold tells the Middle-class that it must do its own work with the help of the State. Culture must be extended on a broad base for all the people. Two things, he said, could be seen: the new movement arising in the Middle-class and the endeavour to get itself established. But the Middle-class must transform itself, said Arnold.

He looked forward to the future when the Middle-class would rule, "liberalised by an ampler culture, admitted to a wider sphere of thought, living by larger ideas, with its provincialism dissipated, its intolerance cured, its pettiness purged away."

The first important point in "A French Eton" is that it shows Arnold unfolding his main ideas. In the 1861 Report there are the seeds, in this work they are selected and developed : the conception of the State derived from Burke as a partnership between members of a society, the aim of education in regard to the nation, and especially the attitude of the three classes of society to culture and ideas ; and most important of all, the need, in order to supply the defect of the Middle-class in culture and ideals, for secondary schools. These are all in the 1861 Report, and developed completely in "A French Eton." "Culture and Anarchy" and "Friendship's Garland" and the separate articles of later years are but expositions of this.

A second important point is that in the year following the publication of " A French Eton " he was appointed to inquire into Secondary Education on the Continent ; and was consulted as to its personnel. (" Letters," Vol. I, page 238.) The style of " A French Eton " is Arnold at his best. It has seriousness, dignity, lucidity ; it is happy in illustrations ; and the concluding portion is noble. It has not the flexibility and grace of his later prose, but it has earnestness and gravity and a certain touch of reality not always present in his later productions. Arnold's own judgment was : " I have written (to my own mind) nothing better " (Letter to his mother, April 29, 1864. " Letters," Vol. I, page 231). " People say it is revolutionary," he wrote to Lady de Rothschild (" Letters," Vol. I, page 232), referring to his anticipation of a day when the working-class would have a " practicable passage to all the joy and beauty of life." How far we have come since then !

(2) Almost immediately after the publication of the third part of " A French Eton " we find that Mr. M. E. Grant-Duff, M.P. (afterwards Sir M. E. Grant-Duff) gave notice of a resolution in the House of Commons urging the necessity of using the endowed schools of the country for secondary education. Then in June, 1865, a Commission under Lord Taunton was appointed to report on Secondary Education in England and Wales.

For this Commission, Arnold was sent to report on secondary and higher education in France, Germany, Switzerland and Italy. As a matter of fact Arnold himself proposed that someone should be sent to study the Continental systems. He appears to have made suggestions as to the first personnel of the Commission. (" Letters," Vol I, page 238.) He set out on this Commission in April 1865, soon after publication of " Essays in Criticism," and returned in October. During this time he saw Paris, Turin, Florence, Rome, Tuscany, Genoa, Milan, Berlin, Baden, Gernsbach, Dresden, Berne, Zurich, and Lucerne. Of people, he saw Guizot, Sainte-Beuve, the Schérers. The " Letters," Vol. I, pages 254 to 308, contain a full record of this interesting journey, in which Arnold first met the rich traditions of Italy.

The Report of this tour was issued in 1868, in a Blue Book, Vol. VI, of the Assistant Commissioners' Report. It was then reprinted in a separate volume with a preface by Arnold. The portion dealing with Germany was again reprinted in 1874, under the title " Higher Schools and Universities in Germany," and that dealing with France was reprinted again in a new edition in 1892, of " A French Eton." The preface to the former is of great length, and is also reprinted in " A French Eton," 82 pages and somewhat irrelevant to the Report which follows. But there are intermittent

discussions of the principles of State action, and
these show signs of Arnold thinking on the basis and
the issues of State action. It is mainly a plea for
the Roman Catholic University for Ireland.
Arnold brings in the two sides of Liberalism which
were opposing this new State-endowment of religion
—Secularist Radicalism represented by J. S. Mill ;
and Nonconformity represented by Mr. Miall
—both united on the ground that the State should
have nothing to do with religion. Arnold charges the
Dissenters with contentiousness and self-assertion.
He states that Pym and his friends were not against
Establishment but against the Establishment of
the Church of England, because it was not the true
religion, that is, it was not their own. Toleration
in the first place they wanted, and equality ; and
the principle of religious equality which Nonconformity has preached Matthew Arnold regards
as the means by which it has really secured its
own ends. This is a clever interpretation, but can
it be said to put the facts justly ? There is some
truth, however, in Arnold's observation that Roman
Catholicism reaches the multitude and especially
the poor, although England does not illustrate it,
and there is justice in his remark that we too often
look at Roman Catholicism from the negative side
only, instead of regarding it as an approximation
to the Truth, and not the Truth any more than
Protestantism is the Truth. Finally the argument

for the Roman Catholic University resolves itself
into the argument for State establishment of religion.

Arnold's position is that religion is too great a
thing to be a matter of voluntary concern but should
be undertaken by the State ; the State establishing
the religion of the majority as expressed in the saying
"The State is of the religion of all its citizens without
the fanaticism of any of them." Arnold cites the
practice of the Continent, Germany, Italy, Switzerland. The great argument which confronts him
is, of course, the political danger, the Ultramon-
tanism involved in the establishment of a Roman
Catholic University. Arnold's reply is, that making
Irish education, as we do, a private hole-and-corner
thing, we drive it to seek connection and attachment
with the larger world in Italy ; whereas this result
would be avoided by the maintenance of a national
Roman Catholic education and a national Roman
Catholic religion. Unfortunately this article is
disfigured at the close by acid references to Dissent;
he attacks its asserted prevention of a religious census, its unattractiveness, its bitter narrowness, and
its essential unreligiousness ; the "greatest obstacle
to our civilisation," these " men of war who have
talked so much of religion " ; in " temper and
contentiousness it (the Nonconformist cause) began,
by temper and by contentiousness it perished." At
the end of all this one asks, What has it to do with
the Report ?

The French Report begins with a history of French secondary schools, that is, the Roman and the Feudal schools of the University of Paris in the Mediæval period, at the Renaissance and during the Revolution. Then follows a history of the changes which occurred under Napoleon I and under the Government of 1830 ; and of the final establishment in 1850 of the present system. This system is then described ; the Imperial Council, the Academic Councils, and the Departmental Councils and the various officials attached to them ; the three kinds of schools under their control ; lycées, communal colleges and private schools. The qualifications and regulations as to teaching are given, and a full account of that most important French institution, the Ecole Normale. The subjects of instruction are outlined, and especially the division into classical and scientific sides. The seven chief classical schools of Paris are described : Arnold notes that the boys looked hardly so healthy as English boys ; and that the French competitive examinations come after the age of fifteen, not at nine or ten as in England. With reference to scholarships he calls particular attention to the advantage of distributing these by a public responsible body instead of local bodies, or what is the usual alternative, after competitive examinations. In France under the joint action of several competent agencies all jobbery in the election is prevented and a more rational application of examination is enforced when examination is decided upon. However, thirty years later, M. Demolins in his book "A quoi tient la supériorité des Anglais," expressly fixes upon the excessive use of competitive examinations as being one of the factors of French inferiority to the Anglo-Saxons. Arnold gives descriptions of several typical schools: the Free School of St. Barbe, Mgr. Cousin's, the Institute Massin, the Communal College of Boulogne, Sainte Géneviève, the Jesuit School at Vaugirard.

In regard to subjects taught, Arnold thought that English public schools were superior in the classics, but the French in mathematics and natural science. Incidentally he criticises the excessive attention in Cambridge to pure mathematics and the retention of Euclid for geometry. In 1867 a law separated in the public schools what we called the modern side from the classical. Distinct examinations, professors, payments, scholarships, programmes were instituted. Arnold was against it but recognised on the Continent the drift towards it. The last chapter of the Report gives an account of superior instruction.

Under this head come the faculties attached to the Academy, and together with auxiliary schools in towns not the seat of the faculty, certain special institutions such as : " The School of Living Oriental Languages." Arnold mentions in comparison with England the superiority of French instruction in Law and Pharmacy.

The recommendations of the Report are entirely in favour of the creation and control by the State of a system of Secondary Education. In Germany Arnold found an even better illustration than in France. But France provides an excellent example. Almost the last word, however, of the Report is a word of criticism. " In France in her superior and still more in her Secondary Instruction there is undoubtedly too much regulation by the Central Government, too much prescribing to teachers the precise course they shall follow, too much requiring of authorisations before a man may stir " (" A French Eton," p. 15). But, as Arnold says, all the salutary and civilising effects of the public establishment of Education are to be had without this.

The original Report is out of print, and we have considered the French portion, as republished in " A French Eton." We now examine the German portion which was published in the volume, " Higher Schools and Universities in Germany."

The Report deals first with the development of schools in Germany, and distinguishes between the Reformation in Germany and in England with regard to classical learning. It gives an account of five classes of Public Secondary Schools ; and the Board of Education by which they are controlled. It describes the organisation of these

schools under School Boards for each town and
District Boards for each district. It describes the
great epoch of Reform initiated by William von
Humboldt when Head of the Education Department and by Wolf at Halle and Berlin.

The special features of the schools, such as the
Abiturienten Examen, are described, the programme
of citizen training, and the general character of
the German system ; such as the public control
of educational endowments, the attention given to
training rather than to examination, the special
teaching on Pedagogy, the lowness of the salaries
and scholarships, in accordance with German
frugality; the three recognised religions, the character of the classical learning of the German pupils,
the special place given to the native literature, and
such gratifying features as at one school where the
pupils have one day every week free for their own
private studies. The results of Arnold's enquiries
are summed up in two most interesting and radical
chapters. Here is treated with great good sense
and vigour the question of classical modern studies.
He adheres firmly to his belief in a superior value
of the classics as mental discipline, but advocates
the adaptation of studies to the aptitudes of the
pupils. Both sides are legitimate portions of
knowledge. Arnold however gives preference to
the teaching of the Humanities, and justifies it in
the following powerful passage :

" The study of letters is the study of the operation of human force, of human freedom and activity ; the study of Nature is the study of the operation of non-human forces, of human limitation, and passivity. The contemplation of human force and activity tends naturally to heighten our own force and activity ; the contemplation of human limits and passivity tends rather to check it. Therefore the men who have had the humanistic training have played, and yet play, so prominent a part in human affairs, in spite of their prodigious ignorance of the Universe ; because their training has powerfully fomented the human force in them."—(" Higher Schools and Universities in Germany," page 158.)

But the interesting point in these last chapters is the sounding of an extraordinary democratic and progressive note. He proposes to found centres of University instruction in the eight or ten largest towns. Oxford and Cambridge are to send professors to them, and for this purpose the University emoluments should be applied. He proposed that the appointment of professors should be taken from Convocation and placed in the hands of an Education Minister upon whom full personal responsibility could be fixed. He proposed that entrance upon any public or professional service should only be open to those who had received for some time superior instruction and had passed its test.

For the Industrial class he desired that instruction

of University order should be organised. This has already been done, not by the State. The University Extension movement has partly carried out Arnold's suggestion of University instruction for the people. To show how far in advance of his time were the Recommendations of the Report, we point to the suggestions for the establishment of a teaching University for London, made effective in 1898.

Indeed on many points it can truly be said that insufficient attention has been given to this Preface, owing perhaps to the fact that it is buried in a technical work. Yet it contains his completest and clearest statement of educational ideas, and their practical application. On the relation of their values of scientific and classical studies on the merits of the several national systems he had studied, on the proposals for our own nation, the last two chapters are the very best summary of Arnold's ideas. The first part of Chapter VIII should be noted, and Chapter IX for the suggestions as to Universities which have since been effected. Once more it should be repeated that the Preface should be considered as the most important and necessary in measuring Arnold's educational work.

(3) Twenty years later he went on a third Commission, to inquire into certain points of elementary education in Germany, Switzerland and France. He commenced work on November

11, 1885, and excluding intervals in England was occupied 14 weeks abroad. The main points of inquiry were : (1) Free Education ; (2) The quality of education ; (3) The status, training and pensioning of teachers ; (4) Compulsory attendance and release from school.

The Report is considerably shorter than the two previous ones, filling only 27 foolscap pages. Arnold's conclusions were : (1) That Continental Education was superior to British ; (2) That British Secondary Education needed to be organised and brought into relation with Primary Education. This latter conclusion is the main aim of the Report, as it is the central aim of nearly everything that Arnold wrote upon Education. From every point he comes to the same goal. In the countries visited he sees the superiority of Primary Education, and traces it first to the better training of teachers and then to the fact that Secondary Education is organised in direct connection with Primary Education. The chief point upon which the Education Department wanted information was the working of Free Education. In 1885 the system established by the Act of 1870 had become settled and the demand for Free Education had arisen. The Report describes in detail the systems in use on the Continent and gives us interesting facts as to the financial conditions in municipalities necessary for the existence of free instruction. After having seen the actual working of the system of free instruction he decides, but not with great emphasis, in favour of payment. He notes these salient points : (1) In France and Switzerland where Education is free the cost falls upon the community, and the advance in Education is itself the cause of free schooling ; (2) In Germany payment is the rule and omission the exception.

Were Free Education to become general it would lead to the establishment of a large number of private schools, because the wealthy have ampler means for the education of their children. To a certain extent this is what has happened in England. However, Arnold concludes with the warning that sooner than that Free Education should become a political partisan question it would be better for a statesman to organise it at once. On this tour Arnold met the Crown Prince and the Princess (later the Emperor and Empress Frederick) and the King of Belgium. He heard Bismarck and he had interviews with Hofmann, Zellar, Mommsen, and Döllinger. The letters written on this visit are peculiarly interesting, and full of manifold interests and delightful expressions of that affection which he possessed so deeply for his family and for his friends.

III. Between the 1868 Report on Higher Education and the 1886 Report on Special Points,

Arnold continued his call for Secondary Schools for the Middle Class in the *Fortnightly Review* in articles dealing with the question in England and Ireland.

> (*a*) July 1878, "Irish Catholicism and British Liberalism."
> (*b*) November 1878, "Porro Unum est Necessarium."
> (*c*) August 1881, " Irish Grammar Schools" (printed in " Irish Essays " under the title "An Unregarded Irish Grievance.")

(*a*) We shall in the study of Arnold's politics examine the article " Irish Catholicism and British Liberalism." It concerns us here as showing his advocacy of Higher Education.

(*b*) In " Porro Unum est Necessarium " Arnold took as his text the Report on Secondary Schools in France since 1865, by the Minister of Public Instruction, M. Bardoux. Strongly as Arnold had urged the organising of Secondary instruction in England, it had not come. He speaks of a " sense of defeat and weakness : "

> " For some twenty years I have been full of this thought, and have striven to make the British public share it with me ; but quite vainly. At this hour, in Mr. Gladstone's programme of the twenty-two engagements of the Liberal Party, there is no word of Middle-Class Education. Twenty-two Liberal engagements,

and the reform of Middle-Class Education not one of them ! What a blow for the declining age of a sincere but ineffectual Liberal. . . ."

M. Bardoux's Report had made Arnold impatient. He gives an account of Secondary Education in France, the number of Lycées, communal schools, écoles libres, and ecclesiastical schools, and the number of scholars. He sums up vividly the comparison of these figures with those of the United Kingdom, 20,000 in the latter to the 157,296 in France. He then describes the superiority of the French middle class, attributing it to (1) The influence of the French principle of Social Equality ; (2) The French system of Secondary Education. Thereupon he takes up the old proposal :

" What is really needed is to follow the precedent of the Elementary Education Act by requiring the provision throughout the country of a proper supply of Secondary Schools, with proper buildings and accommodation, at a proper fee, and with proper guarantees given by the teachers in the shape either of a University degree or of a special certificate for Secondary Instruction."

He outlines the requirements for such a system as to the (a) Provision of means, (b) Teachers, (c) Inspection.

The article " Irish Grammar Schools " was called forth by the publication of Professor Mahaffy's Report upon the Grammar Schools of Ireland in

1879. The Report was a condemnation of three things in the Secondary Instruction system of Ireland:

(1) The competitive examinations ; (2) The condition of the housing of the schools ; (3) The lack of combination and organisation. The Report is made the text for preaching again the Gospel of Secondary Education. He preaches it for Ireland as he preached it for England ; and makes it a part of his proposals for dealing with the Irish question.

In 1874 he published an address which he had given to an Association of Public Elementary Teachers in Westminster on December 6th 1873. Attacks had been made upon the quality of Elementary Education in England. Arnold compares it first with that of America. In America, he says, the provision and maintenance of the schools is better, but the instruction is not. The Continental schools, on the other hand, he admits to be superior and attributes this to the facts : (1) That in England mentality is unawakened ; (2) The continuance of the Middle-Ages ecclesiastical organisation, that is, the Parish ; (3) The system, in England, of payment by result. It is however, the conclusion of the article which should be noticed.

Arnold's educational work, extending over the greater part of his life, can be summarised in a few sentences. 35 years of Inspectorial work, day in,

day out, three Continental tours and the Reports
upon them, and five single articles on Educational
subjects; for Primary Education the Annual
Reports so suggestive in matter, so perfect in style,
permeating by their influence, Code and teaching
and text-book, the Education Act of 1870, Mr.
Forster being Arnold's brother-in-law, and for
Secondary Education the long, continuous, varied
argument and appeal for a State System. With
what truth, therefore, Arnold rested, as he says,
upon that profound verse of the New Testament :

> " So is the Kingdom of God as a man may cast seed
> on to the earth, and may go to bed and get up, night and
> day, and the seed will shoot and extend he knoweth
> not how."

This chapter has been devoted to the technical
side of Arnold's educational work. The larger
reach of this work is considered in his Social
Criticism. But we ought to observe now that
Arnold directly connected the defects of our
Aristocratic and Middle and Working Classes with
our defective system of Education. Hence in
all his work he is moving outwards to the effects
shown in social life of our ideas of Training.
So when he went to America he fixes on American
needs in educational practice. Not only America
but France and Germany are illuminated for the
English mind by their systems of Education. His

daily professional work supplied him with the data of his conclusions, and nothing could be sounder. It is difficult to convey a sense of the wealth of example, of wit, of comparison which he poured out through his pages. Eton to give her boys a Republican fellowship ! Plato, and the meat trade in Chicago! Many of Arnold's proposals have been effected. The State does now direct Education, and daily its directing influence extends. Elementary Education is now compulsory and free. But Secondary Education still lingers. Private Schools are more numerous than ever. Provincial Universities have grown up, but not yet in sufficient numbers. Still the marks of Arnold are in an extraordinary way impressed on the whole nation. Every official utterance is an echo of his voice.

LITERARY CRITICISM

Bibliography

1861. On Translating Homer.
1863. " Dante and Beatrice."
1863. " Essays in Criticism " begun.
1866. On the Study of Celtic Literature begun.
1869. On the Modern Element in Literature.
1869. " Obermann."
1869. " Sainte-Beuve."
1876. " Italian Art and Literature before Giotto and Dante."
1877. Mixed Essays.
1878. " Johnson's Lives."
1879. " Essays in Criticism," Second Series begun.
1882. " An Eton Boy."
1883. Address to the Wordsworth Society.
1885. Discourses in America.
1886. " Sainte-Beuve" (in the " Encyclopædia Britannica).
1888. " Essays in Criticism " (Second Series volume).

ARNOLD was elected to the Chair of Poetry at Oxford in 1857, defeating the Rev. John Ernest Bode. Mr. Herbert Paul points out that Arnold's predecessors in this post were all clergymen, and their successors laymen. The chair was founded in 1708 under the will of Henry Birkhead, Fellow of All Souls and was worth £170 per annum.

The Lectures were delivered in Latin. The post had been held before Arnold by Copleston, Milman, and Keble, and since Arnold, it has been held by Sir Francis Doyle, J. C. Shairp, Palgrave, Courthope, Andrew Bradley, Mackail, Garrod and de Sélincourt. Upon Keble's retirement in 1841 at the height of the Tractarian controversy a keen struggle for the chair took place. On the one side was the Rev. Isaac Williams—described in Froude's " Short Studies on Great Subjects," Vol. IV, p. 258 —a friend of Keble, author of one of the Tracts for the Times, and supported by Dr. Pusey. On the other side the Low Church Party supported the Rev. James Garbett who was eventually elected. Arnold succeeded Garbett's successor, and the chair took on a new life with Arnold. He lectured in English, and excited the academic world with a totally new view of criticism (See *Times*, Feb. 16th, 1911).

The Inaugural Lecture was delivered in 1857. It was published in *Macmillan's Magazine*, Feb. 1869, " On the Modern Element in Literature." It is referred to here as a means of marking the immense development of Arnold's mind. For it is one of the least interesting, least suggestive of Arnold's writings, and shows little promise of the richness to follow. It is a comparison of great periods of national life and their expression in literature. He compares in this connection Greece and Rome with our own Elizabethan period. It is sufficient to say that Arnold delayed the publication for 12 years and never reprinted it. But the Professorship produced first, " On Translating Homer," and then " Celtic Literature."

One feels in reading Arnold's productions that he had pre-eminently the gift for selecting the most engaging parts of his subject, unlike the German method of rigidly treating everything as of equal interest. In these Lectures we feel that Arnold is giving us University lectures upon his professional subject. And we go on to see that the deeper he went into his subject the more interesting he became. " Essays in Criticism " are occupied with the personal element in literature—literature as the revelation of human nature. But here, on Homer, Arnold treats specially of style. The subject which he discusses is the most profound in literature; the essential elements in great literature, and their true expression, that soul and inner aspect of it which makes it edifying, that body and outward aspect of it which makes it charming. Moreover, in choosing a subject from antiquity, and modern translations of it, on the one hand he disengaged himself from all bias as to subject, and on the other hand could show clearly and familiarly the characteristics of fine expression. It is the nearest approach that Arnold ever made to the scientific analysis of style. Analysis we say,

but that analysis which proceeds from the operation
of an infallible taste, rather than a process of the
reasoning faculty.   At the end we feel that we know
what is bad and what is good.   The conclusions
are entirely orthodox.   It would be difficult to rise
from a reading of the book without having firmly
in mind the qualities of the grand style, and that
which distinguishes it from the ballad style.   Nevertheless its pre-eminent value is that it draws the line
between the bad and the good with a master's
hand.   Homer is not the model of all perfect
style ;   he is but the type of one, but to that one
Arnold belonged.   In these lectures he described
and illustrated those very qualities which all his
own writings exhibit.   The lectures consist of
four parts :

(1) Criticism of three versions of Homer.
(2) Criticism of Professor F. W. Newman and
    the ballad-style.
(3) The best method of translating.
(4) Reply to Newman specially describing the
    grand style.

In the first part he sets out the four characteristics
of Homer ;   and treats of Pope, Cowper and Chapman as each failing in one of them.   Homer, says
Arnold, was rapid.   Cowper is not.   Homer,
says Arnold, was simple in style.   Pope is not.
Homer was plain in thought.   Chapman is not.

In the second part he says Homer was noble. Newman is not. He fixes four epithets which Newman
applied to Homer, directly denies them and replaces
them by their opposites. Newman says Homer was
quaint, garrulous, prosaic, low. Arnold says that
he was not. Certainly Arnold was not prosaic.
To say that Newman's version was ignoble, and to
ask with whom he could have lived, not unnaturally
fired Newman. His version no doubts lacks nobleness. Arnold called it the ballad-manner, and free
and easy. He then examines the ballad-manner, as
shown in Chapman, Newman and Maguin ; and
goes on to consider the three possible English
metres for translating Homer. He rejects the
ten-syllabled couplet because of the rhyme, he
rejects blank verse as we know it in Shakespeare
and Milton because it is too complicated. He
commends the hexameter. Dr. Hawtrey had attempted Homer in this and Clough had used it in
his poem, "The Bothie of Tober-na-vuolich."
Arnold then considers the hexameter in relation
to the four qualities of Homer : rapidity, simplicity,
plainness, nobleness. The fourth part, "Last
Words," contains polite references to Newman
which scarcely atone for the attack. It contains
some fine things, a magnificent passage from
Goethe, an aperçu of genius, the necessity for a
prose so perfect that temper or crotchet or erudition may not destroy. How the following judged

Newman ! " He has given, so to speak, full
change for the Greek, but how he gives us our
change; we want it in gold and he gives it us in
copper " (page 119).

The reply is directed against Newman's assertion :
(1) That Homer appeared antiquated to the age of
Pericles; (2) That Homer has obscure places.
Arnold replies that Homer was not antiquated,
but used a poetic diction. He goes on to notice
other criticisms: that Homer was prosaic and low
with his subject. This brings in his exposition of
the grand style. Spedding's attempt to modify
the English hexameter is then noticed, Arnold
keeping to his wish that the English form should
be familiarised. A clear and real distinction
is then made between the simplicity of Tennyson
and that of Homer. Finally Homer is placed not
by his diction and metre, but by the application
of ideas to life. In comparison with him, Arnold
cites the thinness and commonplaceness of ideas
of even the higher balladists such as Scott, and
the lower like Macaulay (p. 172). Incidentally he
expresses belief in the unity of Homer (p. 46). The
treatment of Milton (pp. 72-73) is full of weight
and shows Arnold's judicial power even perhaps
where he had little in common with his author.
The definition of the grand style is one of the most
important parts of the book—" the grand style
arises in poetry when a noble nature, poetically

gifted, treats with simplicity or with severity a serious subject" (p. 138)—and thus fills in the gap which we find in the Milton essay published at the very close of Arnold's life.

Immediately after the lectures on Homer, Arnold began the series of articles which were published with two omissions as the first volume of " Essays in Criticism." An interesting comparison of the two series may be made. The essays of the first volume were among the earliest of Arnold's writings, those of the second volume at the very close. The two series thus stand at the ends of his career, and they enable us to see how the lapse of 27 years of ceaseless thought and production in no sense changed his principles, but brought them to a noble maturity of power. Further it may be noticed that the first volume is occupied almost exclusively with prose writers, and the second, with a few exceptions, is occupied with poets. In the third place the subjects of the first are foreign or classical, and those of the second, with two exceptions, entirely British. Both collections were made by Arnold himself, although the second was published posthumously.

In the first essay of the first volume he speaks of the unity underlying the collection, and what has been said above in comparing the two volumes will suggest that we can study them in their final form better than by the chronological method.

We begin with the first volume which was published early in 1865. It deals mainly, as was said, with foreign and classical literature together with two general articles ; some of the essays having been originally delivered as Lectures from the Chair of Poetry at Oxford. They were published in the following order :

Maurice de Guérin - - -	*January* 1863
Eugénie de Guérin - - - -	- *June* 1863
Heine - - - - - -	- *August* 1863
Marcus Aurelius - - -	*November* 1863
Spinoza - - - - - -	*December* 1863
Joubert - - - - - -	*January* 1864
Pagan and Mediæval Sentiment	- *April* 1864
Literary Influence of Academies	- *August* 1864
Function of Criticism at the present time - - - - -	*November* 1864
A Persian Passion Play - -	*December* 1871

This rapid output of classical work on diverse subjects is remarkable. Especially when we observe that in the same period Arnold published also " A French Eton," Stanley's " Lectures on the Jewish Church," and " Dante and Beatrice." Arnold himself said of " A French Eton " that he had written nothing better; and a severe critic, Professor Saintsbury, gives it unusual praise (" Matthew Arnold," by George Saintsbury, p. 79).

Moreover, at this time he was much occupied with inspecting work, as frequent references in his letters show. The secret of this extraordinarily rapid production of work of the highest rank is expressed in a beautiful passage in a letter to his mother written upon hearing of the death of Thackeray. He wrote, December 24th, 1863 (" Letters," Vol. I, p. 213):

" To-day I am forty-one, the middle of my life in any case, and for me, perhaps, much more than the middle. I have ripened, and am ripening so slowly, that I should be glad of as much time as possible, yet I can feel, I rejoice to say, an inward spring which seems more and more to gain strength, and to promise to resist outward shocks, if they must come, however rough. But of this inward spring one must not talk, for it does not like being talked about, and threatens to depart if one will not leave it in mystery."

Here was the natural source of his power. He had written much of his best poetry and saw it gaining way. He held for the second time the distinction of the Chair of Poetry at Oxford. He had public recognition by his appointment on the 1859 Education Commission. In the report upon this work, and in the lectures on Homer, he had shown a mastery of prose style; with these outward manifestations of his inward grace before us we expect and understand the superb work in the " Essays in Criticism."

They introduced, at least for England, a new kind of criticism. This will be seen by stating the general principle which governed Arnold in his literary judgments. He expressed this principle in a form which cannot be superseded as a statement of the true principles of criticism. He defined criticism as " a disinterested endeavour to learn and propagate the best that is known and thought in the world." Analyse that formula and you have the main lines of Arnold's teaching. This statement consists of three parts :

(1) A disinterested endeavour to learn
(2) And propagate
(3) The best that is known and thought in the world.

The essay, " The Function of Criticism at the present time," is the statement of the need for a sound body of culture, not only for literature, but for the main sphere of national life. Although this is not peculiar to Arnold, there is in his conception more than in others, the idea of selection, the idea of finding and disseminating an edifying literature. Take the essays on the De Guérins, on Joubert, and on Marcus Aurelius, these are more than disinterested estimations of value, they are loving appreciations expressed so as to carry on the light from mind to mind. It is just this missionary aspect of criticism as an endeavour to propagate which fills Arnold's work with an edifying power, and tells upon his readers in the intimate personal way that none of his predecessors ever reached.   This, we say, is what gives to the essays that sense of warmth, of something deep and moral and human.   And then comes next, and great in originality of idea, the third part of Arnold's definition of criticism, " the best that is known and thought in the world."   The following passage exactly expresses the third element:

" . . . the criticism that I am really concerned with —the criticism which can alone help us for the future, the criticism which, throughout Europe, is at the present day meant, when so much stress is laid on the importance of criticism and the critical spirit—is a criticism which regards Europe as being, for intellectual and spiritual purposes, one great confederation, bound to a joint action and working to a common result ; and whose members have, for their proper outfit, a knowledge of Greek, Roman and Eastern antiquity, and of one another. Special, local, and temporary advantages being put out of account, that modern nation will in the intellectual sphere make most progress which most thoroughly carries out this programme."—(" Essays in Criticism," Vol. I, p. 39.)

Europe, one great confederation bound to a joint action and working to a common result, that is the idea in the presence of which Arnold lived.   He brought in Continental judgments, compared them with our current insular ones.   He spread the knowledge of Continental writers.   He added to the limited English outlook wider fields and fresh currents. Of this the first volume of the Essays in Criticism is a clear example. Excluding the two general essays, all the subjects belong to foreign literature : three French, one German, one Dutch, one Roman, one Persian, one classical and one mediæval.

When Arnold wrote, fewer persons had access to Continental literature. The spread of education and means of communication has altered things. There has come to exist in a considerable degree, in spite of the Great War, the European Confederation in which Arnold was, for literature, a pioneer. One can never admit that foreign judgment in literary questions is superior to native. It is that interchange of ideas, mutual sympathy, and above all exact knowledge of the progress of foreign science that is the desideratum. An Englishman will not probably alter his judgment of Shakespeare because of an eccentric French outburst : but he can be, and is, quickened by a touch of the French mind, and perhaps in the contact the French outburst will disappear. In this progress from nationalism to internationalism the eradication of national barriers is taking place to a marked degree in the intellectual sphere. Towards this the recognition and the spread of the sense of a European Confederation was one of Arnold's most fruitful influences.

We now come to another element in Arnold's conception of criticism. It is best described by the word " centrality." The essay on the literary influences of Academies expounds this. The basis of this idea is that there is a standard of the best in literature by which the literary production of a nation must be judged, if it is to be great. This is the use of an institution like the French Academy, which acts as a centre and sets up a standard of correct judgment. The opposite to this is " provinciality," remoteness from the centre. Provinciality, says Arnold, leads to the commonplace in ideas, to exaggeration and the want of that balance secured by the sense of speaking before severe judges. This note of centrality and the scorn of provinciality are the unfailing characteristics of Arnold. Readers will remember how constantly he warns the Dissenters that they are out of the main current of national life, and how humorously and satirically he bring in the opinions of obscure little sectarian journals. The kind of Academy which Arnold wanted has not, and probably will not come. He was more anxious to point out the defects resisted by such an institution, he never earnestly urged the establishment of such institutions ; and in the end his essay on the literary influence of Academies will be treasured rather for its fine examples of urbane criticism.

H

But the distinctive feature and the golden merit of Arnold's criticism lies in his power of perceiving the "admirable riches of human nature." At one time often, and occasionally now, literary criticism has been the dry and technical description of a writer's subject and style. Arnold penetrated into the writer's personality, brought out its gifts of excellence, and showed how literature is but the voice of the spirit. To him the value of a writer was measured by his qualities of nature. The character-judgment was superior to the literary judgment.

Professor Saintsbury, referring to the essays on the De Guérins, is annoyed at the "waste of first-rate power on tenth-rate people." There, we say, is blind criticism ! Who does not see that what fascinated Arnold in the De Guérins was not their literary quality, but their rich and tender spirit, their quality of soul. Admirable riches of human nature ! To hit on these and bring them to light, to make them current and serviceable for thousands of minds, this is what the Essays do. How widely he ranged for treasures, the Roman and Dutch philosophers, the German free-thinker, the Greek poet, the mediæval Christian and the lovely pair of Brittany ! But what treasures he brought ! the touching emotion of Marcus Aurelius beneath the iron exterior of the Roman throne, the thrice-pure philosophy of Spinoza, the moral lucidity of

Joubert, the strange and necessary figure of Heine, the picture of purity and genius in the De Guérins, these are all his revelations of the " admirable riches of human nature." To the judgment of them he brought one standard. He set them high or low by the measure with which they satisfied the moral sense.

There is scarcely a page in the Essays which does not show that the determining consideration in his estimation of a writer was some helpful perception, some guide to conduct, some gift of moral insight, some service to life ; not perhaps such as an untroubled orthodox soul would choose, but which for an enquirer, for an endeavourer, were illuminating and nurturing, when the light of old systems was quenched and the power of old sanctions dissolved. Tenth-rate people, says Mr. Saintsbury. But at least they had reverence and earnestness, and possessed these, wonderful to say, with that subtle quality denied to many righteous, distinction. And then Arnold placed Heine after them. Why ?

" To his intellectual deliverance there was an addition of something else wanting, and that something else was something immense ; the old-fashioned, laborious, eternally-needful moral deliverance. Goethe says that he was deficient in love ; to me his weakness seems to be not so much a deficiency in love as a deficiency in self-respect, in true dignity of character."—(" Essays in Criticism," Vol. I, page 192.)

In Joubert again was Arnold's chance, " the power of his mind and soul at work together in due combination." This is Arnold himself with his intellectual and spiritual penetration. Voltaire, so akin to Arnold in many points, Arnold left alone with Joubert's judgment upon him, " a moral sense in ruins." Reference has been made already to this article; and we shall come to it again when dealing with Arnold's religious and philosophical work, but it is followed by that on Marcus Aurelius. With what sureness he fixes upon the limits which Nature and Fortune had placed upon " one of the best of men." With what sureness he fixed upon the merit of the genius. He points out defects that the power of Marcus Aurelius might be more correctly defined. He seizes on and names the qualities by which Aurelius is immortal. Criticism is here at its best. Here it becomes creative, when by an infallible discrimination it gathers a contagious love and spreads it by the wings of noblest utterance. Mr. George Russell tells us that on the day after the death of Arnold's eldest son he found him with his Marcus Aurelius.

The essay, " Pagan and Mediæval Religious Sentiment," is interesting for its happiness of conception, and the exquisite translation from Theocritus—the conception of the world according to the life of the senses and that according to the heart, with examples taken from Theocritus and

St. Francis; and Heine brought in to set them off. In the 3rd Edition of the " Essays in Criticism " appeared " A Persian Passion Play," a lecture delivered before the Birmingham and Midland Institute, October 16, 1871. It is a curious excursion into an unfrequented path. It is not in Arnold's usual manner, being scarcely more than the paraphrase of a pathetic story of Islam, illustrating his detachment from literary subjects during the period 1867-1877. But it contains a passage on religion of great insight, p. 258. We come back to the expression, " admirable riches of human nature." The main interest in the Essays is life, rather than literature, in man rather than style. Arnold was, as it has been said, an " ardent lover," not a " professional critic." These are the judgments of a mind in close contact with life, and a mind of perfect balance. Further, these judgments are clothed in a conversational style, unfailingly lucid, unfailingly urbane, at times rising into passages of incomparable distinction. Let us name, for example, the "Oxford passage," and the conclusions of the Eugénie de Guérin and Marcus Aurelius essays.

These essays are the whole of Arnold's literary work in 1863-1864, except two others, one entitled " The Bishop and the Philosopher," now partly included in the essay on Spinoza, in the " Essays in Criticism " Vol. I, and one on Dean Stanley's

" Lectures on the Jewish Church," *Macmillan's Magazine* February 1863—which we shall study later—and one on Dante and Beatrice, *Fraser's Magazine* May 1863. Of the latter we have no information, except that in one of his letters Arnold says that it was an old lecture, "Letters," Vol. I, p. 185. He wrote only two pieces on Italian literature, a short preface and this article. Mr. Theodore Martin (later Sir Theodore) had recently published a translation of Dante's Divine Comedy, in which he represented Dante's love for Beatrice as a real love—a passion and not a spiritual ideal. Arnold points out the difficulties that confront this theory. Both married ; Mr. Martin settled this by saying that Dante buried his regrets with his heart ; and that Gemma Donna was quite content with the affection of a second love ! Arnold's compromise is that the Beatrice of Dante's youth became the basis of his spiritual ideal.

". . . symbolises for him the ineffable beauty and purity for which he longs. Even to Dante at twenty-one, when he yet sees the living Beatrice with his eyes, she already symbolises this for him, she is already not the ' creature not too bright and good ' of Wordsworth, but a spirit far more than a woman ; to Dante at twenty-five composing the ' Vita Nuova ' she is still more a spirit ; to Dante at fifty, when his character has taken its bent, when his genius has come to its perfection, when he is composing his immortal poem, she is a spirit altogether."—(*Fraser's Magazine*, May, 1863, page 669.)

There is a curious, grave earnestness in Arnold's treatment of the theme. One wonders how with such a situation the author of Friendship's Garland could have controlled his humour. The "Dante and Beatrice" has recently for the first time been reprinted. It has not the general applications of Arnold's thought, but it is a unique example of his gift of judgment applied to a single and limited subject. And the conclusion which we give above is in Arnold's perfect style. He omitted it from the "Essays in Criticism," although it was written with the other Essays of the first volume. But it was four years before a second edition was printed.

The "Essays in Criticism" were collected and published in 1865. In this year he was occupied with his work as an Education Commissioner. In 1866 he gave his second course of Oxford Lectures in the Chair of Poetry. They were on Celtic Literature and were published separately in the *Cornhill* in 1866, together in 1867. "Hardly the sort of book a British parent buys at a railway book-stall for his Jemina," said Mr. Geo. Smith to Arnold. At this time the old Irish literature between 700 and 1200 A.D., was being made accessible through the labours of a number of scholars, here and on the Continent. The main historical and geographical lines were laid down by Eugene O'Curry and John O'Donovan, and the grammar was studied particularly in Germany. Later, and especially since the date of Arnold's lectures, a great number of manuscripts have been published. With his eye, as usual, in a practical direction Arnold describes the effect of ethnological science upon religion and politics. In religion it tends to establish the divergence between the Indo-European and the Semitic races. In politics it tends to abate the enmity between Great Britain and Ireland. Arnold goes on to state the quantity of Celtic Literature extant. (It is curious that he did not know any of the Celtic tongues.) He takes the fair position against such negative critics as Mr. Nash that while we must admit the late origin of much so-called Celtic writing, yet a large basis of genuine work is left. The sceptical position is that all Celtic civilization perished at the time of Paulinus A.D. 59, and that the manuscripts extant belong to the Welsh revival of the 12th and 13th centuries. On the other side Arnold states the line of evidence of the existence of an old national literature. Zeuss's work, then quite recent—his Grammatica Celtica was published in 1853—establishing the age of the different groups of Celtic writing, is described ; and the general results of philology in proving the kinship of Celt and Teuton. Then comes a slight reference to the physiological evidence of the Celtic element, and after this, the last part of the book, the pencilling of the three elements, the Saxon, the Norman and the Celt. This is the heart of the book, and Arnold's genius works here at its best : the clearness of the sight, the light which he lets in, the delicate discrimination, the sense of the judgment of national character by a spirit, by a perfectly poised judge.

That Arnold fixed on real distinctions of characteristics is certain, but that these are to be traced entirely to the sources he selects is perhaps not so certain. In a sense, if the actual fact be observed, he made a Celtic element, and in future such traits must be known as Celtic. Only a pedant will try to verify in each detail the delineation of the mental physiognomy of the Celt. The groups and cast of qualities which Arnold fixed on are real and familiar. The historical origin of each of the elements which he describes may be after all uncertain, but in the main and in regard to practice, Arnold's analysis was a true one, it was natural.

The most important parts of the Lectures were Parts Five and Six; the first describing the modification of the German elements in use in rhetoric and religion by the Celtic, the sixth reaching the centre of the subject, the Celtic element in poetry. However, Arnold does not follow closely the development of the theme, and after showing the Celtic element in rhetoric and religion—the scantiest attention is given to this—gives an interesting, if cruel, account of the German temperament. He compares the Celtic gift of quick observation with the slow, steady German " going steadily along close to the ground."

In English poetry he makes out the Celtic influence to be that shewn by three things—its style, melancholy, and its natural " magic " in rendering Nature. He illustrates the first by comparing English with German literature. Goethe perceived the lack of this element, and " laboured all his life to impart style into German literature." Arnold illustrates this further by comparing the German Nibelungen and our own hymnody. In contrast with these, as each showing the Celtic genius for style, he introduces Welsh and Irish epitaphs.

Of the Celtic melancholy he wrote :

> " The Celts with their vehement reaction against the despotism of facts, with their sensuous nature, their manifold striving, their adverse history, their immense calamities, the Celts are the prime authors of this vein of piercing regret and passion—of the Titanic in poetry."—(Page 127.)

To verify this comes in Ossian, and to show it in English, Byron. On the third, " the gift of rendering with wonderful felicity the magical charm of Nature," Arnold is most happy.

We will not here follow Arnold in his analysis. On his familiar method of contrasts, the four ways of rendering Nature are described in order to

set out distinctly the fourth, the magical way of
rendering Nature ; the eye on the object but
charm and magic added, as Arnold defined it.
There is no need to discuss his assertion as to the
origin of this.   The treatment itself is too charming
to be argued with.   The unerring choices, the
humorous banter of the Teuton, the butterfly
flitting from flower to flower carries entire admiration.   It is impossible to regard the lectures
as Science.   They could not possibly establish
any conclusions.   Since   " Celtic   Literature "
appeared there has been a Celtic Renaissance.
The Chair of Celtic was established at Oxford.
Reprints of original works from Brittany, Wales
and Ireland have appeared until a large library of
Celtic remains has been accumulated.

An immensity of Celtic material is now available
which was not known in Arnold's time.   To this
one of Arnold's pupils at Oxford, Sir John Rhys,
has made considerable contributions.   It was
Arnold's genius that hit on the possibilities of Celtic
study.   He led the way and his Lectures may be
regarded as the Introduction to the Celtic Movement
of recent years.

Yet the discovery of this new material has only
confirmed the soundness of Arnold's judgment.
Mr. Alfred Nutt, in his edition of " Celtic Literature," has contested Arnold's statement that the
Celts reacted against the despotism of facts.   He

says that Arnold based the statement on the Welsh
Llywarch Hen and on Ossian ; but that the former
was not typical of Celtic Literature in general and
that Ossian simply reflected the fashionable sentiment of his day.   Again Mr. Nutt says that Arnold
illustrated this quality of the Celtic temperament—
its Titanism—from Byron.   But Byron, says Mr.
Nutt, is the least Celtic of the great English poets.
Shelley was the better example.   Arnold cites the
French as illustrating the Celtic temperament.   But
this Mr. Nutt denies.   The question turns on the
existence in genuinely Celtic literature of the revolt
against the despotism of fact.   Mr. Nutt's interesting observations on pp. 85-87 (Note, " Celtic
Literature " [David Nutt]) should be read.

" Celtic Literature" was published in 1867.
For the next ten years Arnold followed other lines.
" Culture and Anarchy, " Literature and Dogma,"
" St. Paul and Protestantism," and some of his most
popular works.   Literature he left alone.   This
is the period which Mr. Saintsbury calls " In the
Wilderness."   For in it he produced his theological
writings.   Mr. Saintsbury does not care for these.
Tastes differ.   He prefers Arnold only in literature.

The only pure literature of the period was a few
slight pieces which we may note.   Two short
articles written in the first and second numbers of
the *Academy*, October and November, 1869, on
Obermann and on Sainte-Beuve.   That on Ober-

mann is not important. Arnold had already
published his two poems on Obermann, and no
prose could make clearer his spiritual debt to De
Sénancour. The short piece here is simply descriptive. That on Sainte-Beuve, published just
before the latter's death, is more to be missed.
He fixes among other things on Sainte-Beuve's
unprejudiced reception of fact—the naturalist in
literature. He states too the judgment that Sainte-
Beuve stopped short at curiosity and failed to make
the larger applications of his knowledge.

The "Persian Passion Play" essay in "Essays
in Criticism," was first published in the *Cornhill
Magazine*, December, 1871. He wrote too, a
short preface to "Lectures on Italian Art and
Literature, before Giotto and Dante," by Edoardo
Fusco. This was printed in *Macmillan's Magazine*,
1876. Fusco was a teacher of Italian and Modern
Greek in London, in 1854-1859, and later a Professor
at Naples. Arnold met him again in 1865 at
Naples. The Introduction is slight, but contains
an interesting comparison in defining civilisation
between Dante and Goethe. Very interesting in
view of the events which have happened since
1914.

In 1877 came a new series, a return to literature,
the essays collected in "Mixed Essays." Thence-
forward to the end Arnold produced about one
piece in literature every year. The political pieces

of " Mixed Essays " we will take in another place,
and the literary contents in their time order.

The mere titles of the pieces suggest the catho-
licity of Arnold's mind. A personal and
enthusiastic tribute to George Sand by the side
of the Milton paper ; Goethe through the eyes of
Schérer. Thus the sense of the European judgment is present again, as in the first volume of
" Essays in Criticism." Superbly English as
Arnold was in many of his qualities, his intellectual
orthodoxy was not distorted. The wide capacity
of his admirations gave to his judgments something
of an international character.

The earliest of these papers is the Milton. It
contains the well-known ascription of the " grand
style " to Milton. In this respect Arnold placed
Shakespeare below Milton, basing his judgment on
Milton's unfailing sureness in diction and rhythm.
On this it may be said that a work must draw its
character from the subject. Shakespeare dealt
with the whole of humanity, both in its grandeur
and in its pettinesses. Milton moved in a different
world. Most people will agree that Milton maintained an unfailing height of style, but Shakespeare
was no less the master of his great subject, becoming
more than the great and less than the little.

A second feature of the Milton paper is the
insistence upon truth in literary admiration. The
pleasure from the author must actually be realised

by the reader.   Conventional judgment is nothing.
This doctrine, stated on p. 250 in " Mixed Essays,"
2nd Edition, is quite consistent with Arnold's
underlying ideas of certain standard judgments.
It certainly establishes liberty for variety of appreciation.   Some great names in literature bore me.
They should.   Every great writer has to be appro-
priated by the individual.   With this doctrine
of personal verification of literary judgment must
be taken the comparative method which Arnold
constantly used; comparison of critic with critic,
of country with country, of author with author.
It is in this that he placed the corrective to eccentricities of personal taste.   Taken together the
doctrine of personal verification and comparison
constitute something like the inductive method in
literature.   The force and value of Arnold lie in
the combination of these.   Isolated they lead
astray.   Personal appreciation and standard judgments are complementary.

" Falkland" appeared just after, in March
1877.   The " Falkland " article might very well
be separated from this literary group and placed in
a small but significant class of Arnold's writings
devoted to expositions of temper, of manner, of
quality of mind.   With it should be placed
the " A Speech at Eton " on Flexibility, and
" A Liverpool Address " on Lucidity, for these
are distinctive expressions of Arnold's temperament.

He praised in " Falkland " amiability.   The immediate cause of the article was finely and boldly
expressed.   " It is proposed to raise, on the
field of Newbury, a monument to a famous Englishman who was amiable."   The Puritans were
not attractive to Arnold, and Falkand is set off
against Hampden.   There could be no sympathy
between Arnold and the harsh, fighting insistency
of the Parliamentarians, and there comes a shot
at the Philistine of genius in religion, Luther and
the Philistine of genius in politics, Cromwell and
the Philistine of genius in literature, Bunyan.

We will leave " Mixed Essays " at this point
for the sake of following the three pieces mentioned
above.

In the *Cornhill Magazine*, May, 1879, appeared
" A Speech at Eton," really an address to the
Eton Literary Society.   The article was reprinted
in " Irish Essays," 1882.   It is in the main a
pæan for a quality praised by the Greeks, eutrapelia,
translated by Arnold as " happy and gracious
flexibility."   Apart from the article being an interesting instance of Arnold's method, selecting a
single word and tracing its history, it belongs
to this group of writings which expresses one of the
main characteristics of Arnold himself, and further
it connects itself naturally with the main current of
his teaching.   There are several lines of development of the human spirit, and progress is to be made

harmoniously along each—happy and gracious flexibility.

With this Eton address we may join the article " An Eton Boy," *Fortnightly Review*, June 1882. It is a slight in-memoriam account of an Eton boy, Arthur Clynton Baskerville Mynors, whose diaries, published privately, came into Arnold's hands. He at once fixed on the educational interest of such a life as Mynors, in its reflection of the effect of Eton training. What is specially noticeable is the handsome tribute to the indispensable virtues produced by English Puritanism.

In November of the same year was published " A Liverpool Address," an address at the opening of the session of University College, Liverpool. Just as he had preached Amiability in Falkland, and Flexibility in the " Eton Address," he has singled out Lucidity as the great want of the English nation. Lucidity he defines negatively as the perception of the want of truth and validity in systems and ideas long current. His two exponents of lucidity are Luther and Voltaire. The practical hit of Arnold of course comes on. Lucidity, had we it, would destroy for instance the Salvation Army, would destroy the Ritualist movement. So he preaches lucidity and advises the educational centres to generate the spirit of lucidity.

Here let us return to " Mixed Essays." George

I

Sand died June 8th, 1876. The article on her immediately began to take shape in Arnold's mind, and was published in June 1877. He writes to Miss Arnold in June, 1876:

> "I also heard from Morley yesterday that George Sand had said to Renan that when she saw me years ago, 'Je lui faisais l'effet d'un Milton jeune et voyageant.' Renan told him this. Her death has been much in my mind ; she was the greatest spirit in our European world from the time that Goethe departed."

At a later date than the first visit he was less inclined to go and see her—" to take so long a journey to see such a fat old Muse," as a French friend said to him. ("Letters," Vol. I, p. 106.) The interest of the article lies in the records of the *first* visit to George Sand in 1846, when he was 22. He was then plainly an enthusiast for her teaching ; and his account of her work—the passion of agony and revolt, the consolation from Nature and from beauty, the ideas of Social renewal—are unmistakably characteristics of Arnold's work. He was therefore going back to his past and tracing the origins of his own intellectual life. There was very little of passion and revolt in Arnold, as he wrote. He was 55, and his place in public judgment well established. One of his paragraphs opens with the beautiful passage : " Joy is the great lifter of men, the great unfolder." Mature

and happy and easy expression we shall find nowhere
better shown than in this essay.

In the same year, December 1877, appeared
" A Guide to English Literature." This is a
Review of Mr. Stopford Brooke's " A Primer of
English Literature." It recommends the book
and adds a few critical suggestions. There again
appears Arnold's somewhat critical appraise-
ment of Shakespeare. To the subjects incidentally treated we shall come again in the second
volume of the " Essays in Criticism."

The last of the literary papers appearing in
" Mixed Essays "—which we have been considering
in the order of their first publication—was " A
French Critic on Goethe," January 1878. It
is practically a reproduction of M. Schérer's criticism
of Goethe, following Schérer rather closely. There
is the same excellent and instructive comparison
of national points of view. An Englishman
is writing on a Frenchman's judgment of a German.
Incidentally Arnold again reveals his estimate of
Shakespeare—for his mention of Schérer's reference
amounts to assent—Schérer having said that whereas
Shakespeare had more power than Goethe, the latter
had the greater range. What is interesting in the
essay is the careful balancing, and the comparisons
of criticisms. The whole effect is to arrive at conclusions of something like justness and finality.

We have now completed our survey of the literary

portion of the volume, " Mixed Essays." It has
already been said that Arnold's work on literary
subjects was continuous. The Goethe paper in
" Mixed Essays " appeared about the same time
as Arnold's selection of Johnson's " Lives of the
Poets." The Introduction to this is one of his
most valuable pieces. In the manner of setting
forth the status of the work he was editing, and in
explaining the use of such a selection it is unexcelled.
In the Introduction to Isaiah, chaps. 1-40, he had
already explained his method of *points de repère*.
Here he carries the same principles into literary
history. The method itself is priceless ; it marks
the difference between a master and a bungler.
If a man does not get hold of these *points de repère*,
natural centres, he is useless, and his erudition
is an obstruction to other minds, while to have them
is lucidity, is generalising, is science. Arnold's
selection was first of first-class writers and then of
these with a definite period. The Lives are interesting enough and will repay re-reading at all times.
It is refreshing and stimulating once again to see
the light radiating out from Johnson's sound
mind over the literary ground. With all its
irreverence is it all pain to be reminded of Johnson's
view of Lycidas, " how one god asks another
god what has become of Lycidas, and how neither
god can tell"? Arnold placed his finger, to use his
expression, on Johnson's chief merit, his prose

organism (did he mean organ ?), that service of his to his age which turned a prose " cumbersome, unavailable, impossible," into one of regularity, uniformity, precision, balance. Arnold sets out with just force Johnson's misfortune in that he lived in an age when poetry was low. " Johnson was the man of an age of prose." Johnson and Arnold on the intellectual side were not unlike. That which is characteristically English, sound sense, distrust of the sentimental, the firm grasp of the practical, both had to a marked degree. They were alike in the recognition which has been accorded to them as censors of national life and of individual character. But the Johnsonian traits in Arnold limited his appreciations ; as we shall see in the case of his estimate of Wordsworth.

Arnold's strictly literary work after the Introduction to the " Lives " is for the most part comprised in one or two essays republished in " Irish Essays," 1882, and in two volumes, the Second Series of " Essays in Criticism," published after his death, but prepared by himself, and issued with a short notice by Lord Coleridge; and the volume, " Discourses in America." To these we may add the article in the " Encyclopædia Britannica," October 1885. In point of time the essays are in two periods and the Discourses come in between. Of the contents of " Irish Essays " written at this time we may notice " The French Play in London,"

Nineteenth Century, August 1879. A company of French actors and actresses, Sarah Bernhardt among them, appeared at the Gaiety Theatre, and this provided Arnold with matter for a comparison of French and English dramatic literature. The theme is that a nation with the highest poetical genius has its adequate poetical form. He then says that the French Alexandrine prevented Molière from being in the rank of the greatest, and so too Racine and Corneille.

But the main plea of the piece is for a national theatre ; "The theatre is irresistible : organise the theatre," is the injunction. A State-aided Company, and in addition a School of Elocution, that was the proposal, as in Education Arnold had advocated what must gladden every socialistic mind, State Control. The State is to act in its corporate and collective character even in the sphere of national manners through the theatre. It is interesting to note that this Essay, out of his track as it is, has been selected as one of the best examples of his prose.

I take the Essays in order of time first, and then the Discourses. The second volume of Essays is a revelation of Arnold's ascending power. Diction, style and sureness of experience all shine forth with greater and greater lucidity. It is one more proof that the trained mind goes from strength to strength while the untrained genius frequently blazes forth for a short space and then collapses.

In the Essays, then, we come first to the article on

Wordsworth contributed as a Preface to an edition of Wordsworth of 1879, in Messrs. Macmillan's Golden Treasury Series. Wordsworth was a neighbour and friend of the Arnold family at Fox How. It is, therefore, a great thing that Arnold with his critical justness could raise and place Wordsworth so high as next after Shakespeare and Milton in England, and next after Goethe in Germany, and next after Molière in France. How far it is possible to assess achievement in different literatures is difficult to say, and by no means so easy to decide as Arnold apparently found it. He was just then fully occupied in the European atmosphere, the work on Goethe and Schérer having recently appeared. In this introduction is a passage expressing one of Arnold's chief doctrines :

"Let us conceive of the whole group of civilised nations as being, for intellectual and spiritual purposes, one great confederation, bound to a joint action and working towards a common result : a confederation whose members have a due knowledge both of the past, out of which they all proceed, and of one another. This was the ideal of Goethe, and it is an ideal which will impose itself upon the thoughts of our modern societies more and more. Then to be recognised by the verdict of such a confederation as a master or even as a seriously and eminently worthy workman, in one's own line of intellectual or spiritual activity, is indeed glory ; a glory which it would be difficult to rate too highly."—(" Essays in Criticism," Vol. 2, p. 126-127.)

He thus places Wordsworth, and we must now see the moving reason in Arnold's mind. He takes up again the doctrine stated in the " Homer Lectures " that " the noble and profound application of ideas to life is the most essential part of poetic greatness." Wordsworth exemplified this. To the question which most interests every man—How to live ?—he gave an answer. With quiet force and precision Arnold asserted his view that great poetry is not where the form is studied and exquisite, is not poetry of revolt against moral ideas, is not poetry of indiffer- ence. Wordsworth dealt with life. Thus Voltaire, Heine, Keats, Gautier all stand aside. Then the Wordsworthians come in for criticism. They praise him for the wrong things. Criticism in general will go with him here, and will say that Wordsworth's philosophy is not so incontestably sound as his disciples say. Wordsworth's greatness lies in that he " feels the joy offered to us in Nature, the joy offered to us in the simple primary affections and duties." " Nature herself seems," said Arnold, " to take the pen out of his hand, and to write for him with her own bare, sheer, penetrating power " (p. 158). The praise rendered to Wordsworth was great and effective. It elucidated Wordsworth and introduced him to a larger world of readers.

But Arnold lacked the transcendental tempera- ment, and in this respect failed to set forth that side of Wordsworth ;   he had the Johnsonian quality of plain, practical common-sense, but had little appreciation of the mystical world.   Wordsworth's poetry, on the other hand, undoubtedly had the mystical quality.   No one better than Arnold set out the beauty and power of Wordsworth's expression of Nature's joy-giving power.   But he scarcely did justice to the transcendental philosophy which gave unity to his poetry.   This was undoubtedly a defect in Arnold's estimate of Wordsworth.   But it must be observed that his mode of criticism was essentially selective, that is, that it set out to disengage certain, and not all, of the points of his subject.   His was not a complete inventory of them, but a choice description of the unmistakably excellent in them.

Probably as a result of this selection of Wordsworth, and in spite of the gentle criticisms of the Wordsworthians, he was elected President of the Wordsworth Society, and on May 2, 1883, gave a Presidental Address.   A letter referring to this event is worth reproduction here.

" The speech is over and I got through pretty well. The grave would have been cheerful compared to the view presented by the Westminster Chamber and the assembled Wordsworth Society when I came upon the platform.   The hall was not full, the worthy ———— having rather muddled things, and the Society is not composed of people of a festive type.   But my darling

Lucy looked charming, and so did Ally, who came with her. Coleridge, who proposed a vote of thanks to me, was very sweet. The papers were awfully boring, except Stopford Brooke's, which was saved by his Irish oratorical manner. I have quite been bilious for the last day or two, and to-day, when I saw the Society drawn out before me, my tongue clave to the roof of my mouth, and I nearly began to retch."—("Letters," Vol. II, p. 211.)

The address was published in *Macmillan's Magazine*, June 1883, and reprinted in *Words-worthiana*, 1880. It is pure Arnold—the Wordsworth Society as a monastery, the "endeavour to keep what little leisure I can for reflexion and amendment before the inevitable close," the beautiful introduction of Vergil at the close. There is, too, most noticeable the distinct presence of thoughts of the end, although separated from it by five years.

In 1880, Arnold contributed a General Introduction to the selections from Gray and Keats, in T. H. Ward's "English Poets." The General Introduction contains some of Arnold's best explanatory work. It adopts again his touchstone method: and it is noticeable for a full treatment of Burns. The estimate of Chaucer is valuable. But the main weight of it is in the description of the characteristics of great poetry. Define it Arnold will not, but only gives the qualities by which we may recognise it. According to his summary the chief points are, truth and seriousness in the matter,

loftiness of diction and movement in the style.
The Introduction is a review of English poets by
the test of this standard.   The reader should par-
ticularly notice the fullness of Arnold's diction.
His mastery of language was still growing.
Of this we give the following specimen :

> " And yet Chaucer is not one of the great classics.
> His poetry transcends and effaces, easily and without
> effort, all the romance poetry of Catholic Christendom :
> it transcends and effaces all the English poetry contem-
> porary with it, it transcends and effaces all the English
> poetry subsequent to it down to the age of Elizabeth.
> Of such avail is poetic truth of substance, in its natural
> and necessary union with poetic truth of style.   And yet,
> I say, Chaucer is not one of the great classics.   He
> has not their accent."—(" Essays in Criticism," Vol. II,
> pp. 31-32.)

The Keats essay is short but full of surprises.   It
commences with a chilly disparagement of Keats,
for his vein of sensuousness and for his indolence,
but ends with a most noble eulogy.   The severe
demand for the moral element which was the mark
of Arnold's judgments appears again.   What
weighed for good in Arnold's mind was Keats'
worship of Beauty in all its forms.   It was this
mighty formative power which redeemed Keats
from the charge of mere sensuousness.   Arnold
describes his work as Shakespearean.   He does
this because of Keats' magical interpretation of

Nature : and because of Keats' "rounded perfection and felicity of loveliness of expression."

The essay on Gray is not important. It deals
with the purely personal aspect of Gray and does
not raise the great questions of literature. It
contains the usual single expression, either Arnold's
own or selected, summarising his ideas. Of Keats :
"He is with Shakespeare," Of Gray : "He
never spoke out."

We pass on to the Byron Introduction, which
stands as a perfect model. It is intensely interesting
from opening to close : it is marked with memorable
passages, and lays down a judgment of Byron which
for current times is final. This is worth noting, and
proves the detachment of Arnold's mind. For
Arnold could have had little sympathy of temperament with Byron. Byron's excesses, the formless-
ness of his art, must have repulsed Arnold. Yet
his judgment is quite impersonal. Both his
praise and blame secure general and instant recognition. He praised him sincerely, and one feels the
source and measure of his appreciation exactly.

The essay contains a curious prophecy as to the
position of Byron and Wordsworth in the year
1900. It can hardly be said to have been fulfilled,
certainly not for Byron. The star of poetry has been
clouded by the political storms which have raged
in the latter part of the 19th century, and pales
in the scientific light of the 20th century.

In the 2nd Vol. of " Essays in Criticism," there was a space of time between the Byron Introduction and the Amiel paper which comes next. In that period Arnold went on his American tour. Shelley naturally follows Byron, and we take Arnold's essay on him first. Prof. Dowden's " Life of Shelley " was the immediate cause. That book inevitably drew attention to the personal aspect of Shelley. Hence the view which one gets is extremely disagreeable. The personal estimate was always present in Arnold's literary judgments : it was present in his judgment of Byron, but there was present also a full recognition of Byron's work. The " Shelley " essay does not give this impression. On the personal matters the contempt is superbly just, and the passage, " What a set, what a world " will remain against Shelley for ever, but Shelley's genius requires other recognition. How could Arnold deal with it ? He could not enter into Wordsworth's transcendentalism ; he could not grasp Shelley's impalpable, intangible creations. The world of imagination so real to Shelley was unknown to Arnold. The intuitive perception of meaning, the natural sympathy of mind were absent, and hence we have a view of Shelley on the dark side—the resplendent and heavenly genius is only half seen. Lord Coleridge asserted that Arnold intended to write on Shelley something more. But the Byron Introduction was written seven years before, and in that Arnold suggested that Shelley's essays and letters would stand higher than his poetry.

The essays on Amiel and on Tolstoi were published after the American tour, just before the Shelley review. It was natural that Arnold, who had steeped himself in Obermann, should eventually come upon Amiel. The difference is that he was 27 when he wrote the stanzas on Obermann and 65 when writing the review of Amiel. Life lay between. Hence the change in tone. The clinging fascination of youth remains, and it is clear that Obermann held the greater place in Arnold's mind. Moreover, his practical instincts turned away from the philosophical speculations of Amiel, just as we have seen they did from Wordsworth and from Shelley. It is fairly certain that his interest in the Introspective school survived in him, but it is also certain that it had been superseded in his mind. Ideas to work with, ideas to live with, this was the test for Arnold. He insists on the need for limit and for the feasibility of performance.

The article on Tolstoi (*Fortnightly Review*, December, 1887) is a description of his novel, Anna Karénine. It may be considered as one of the least interesting of Arnold's works. Its greatest interest is in showing how late Arnold was in advancing on to fresh ground. The thread of sympathy between them lies in Tolstoi's rendering of the inward religion of Jesus Christ.

The last in time of the second series of " Essays
in Criticism " is the address on Milton, given in
St. Margaret's Church, Westminster, on the 13th
February 1888, two months and two days before
his death.   Arnold's single subject is the influence
of Milton, through his use of the grand style,
and his undeviating standard of excellence.   What
is noteworthy in this short piece is the sign of
the still increasing richness of Arnold's own
diction, the still increasing ease of style up to the
end.   There is, too, the characteristic flavour of
audacity in it.   A memorial window to Milton in
St. Margaret's Church was being unveiled ; it
was the gift of an American.   Hence the gentle
reference to the Anglo-Saxon contagion, and the
Anglo-Saxon flood which will beat against the
grand style in vain.   It may be well to note here
that Arnold owed much to Milton.   He owed much
in style, in diction, and in the distinctly classical
cast of his poetry.   Many suggestions and phrases,
and many conceptions of persons, may be traced to
Milton.   Let the reader as a proof read Arnold's
" Thyrsis," and then Milton's " Comus."

We now come to the American Discourses.
Arnold landed in New York, in 1883, and returned
in February 1884.   He prepared three lectures
for the tour which are now published in the volume,
" Discourses in America."   They were prepared
with great care, the second, " Literature and

Science " being the Rede Lecture at Cambridge.
(Published in the *Nineteenth Century*, 1882, and republished in the " Discourses in America.") Of
" Numbers " he wrote : " I have nearly broken
my heart over my first discourse." (" Letters,"
Vol. II, p. 213.)   His letters before and during this
trip are intensely engaging.   They show hard
work, constant pondering, and the gradual growth
of the work.   Yet the result is easy and flowing
and free from apparent effort.

In " Numbers " he turned his critical powers away
from personal estimates like those of Byron and
Shelley to surveying whole nations.   He compared France and the United States and England.
His method of arranging the subject is perfectly
clear.   Selecting phrases out of the great inclusive
ideal of St. Paul, " Whatsoever   things   etc.,"
he applies them to each country in turn ;   to
England and its treatment of Ireland, " Whatsoever
things are amiable."   But the main theme is
France and the worship of Lubricity.   What he
said later in the Shelley Essays he says here with
force against France.   He says it with emphasis,
and one feels that he is speaking with conviction.
" Whatsoever things are elevated "—nobly serious
—is the reference for America.   Behind it all is
the doctrine of Isaiah, the doctrine of the " remnant"
who are to redeem the nation.   The discourse on
" Numbers " is typical of Arnold.   It is the Arnold

gospel, and strictly the continuation of "Literature and Dogma."

"Literature and Science" was a Rede Lecture at Cambridge, 1882, published in the *Nineteenth Century*, August, 1882, and re-prepared for the American tour. It is a simple and direct statement of the case for letters as against the claims of some scientists, Prof. Huxley in particular. The opposition between the two is still felt, but certainly not so acute as at this time. Arnold's ground is that there exist in men various senses, the sense for conduct, for beauty, for social manners, for knowledge. Science will only satisfy the sense for knowledge, leaving the others unfulfilled. Arnold's contentions will now probably be admitted. Moreover he thought that powers of observation and comparison were better developed by the Natural Sciences, e.g. Botany, than by verifications of the law of Grammar. From a literary man, the following is interesting as showing that at least Arnold had an unprejudiced mind on the question. Writing to Mrs. Forster (January, 1866),—he says:

"If it is perception you want to cultivate in Florence, you had much better take some science (Botany is perhaps the best for a girl, and I know Tyndall thinks it the best of all for educational purposes) and choosing a good handbook, go regularly through it with her. Handbooks have long been the great want for teaching the natural sciences, but this want is at last beginning

K

to be supplied, and for Botany a textbook based on Henslow's Lectures, which were excellent, has recently been published by Macmillan. I cannot see that there is much got out of learning the Latin Grammar except the mainly normal discipline of learning something much more exactly than one is made to learn anything else ; and the verification of the laws of grammar in the examples furnished by one's reading, is certainly a far less fruitful stimulus of one's powers of observation and comparison than the verification of the law of a science like Botany in the examples furnished by the world of nature before one's eyes."—(" Letters," Vol. I, p. 313.)

Reading the lecture to-day it seems out of date. Later advocates of letters and later scientists modify their claims and have thus largely removed the antagonism. What is left is the antagonism of temperament. This lecture is an example, rare enough, of Arnold fighting in the serious mood. The customary persiflage, the dilettante handling, disappear, and in place come downright blows— powerful because not more than true.

The third of the Discourses is on Emerson. What the reader feels first is the unique grace and ease and lucidity of Arnold's method of laying out the subject. The interesting personal opening, then all the criticism which can be laid against Emerson, then the turning point, " And now I have cleared the ground, I have given up to envious Time as much of Emerson as Time can fully

expect ever to obtain " (p. 178). So he prepares
the way for the enumeration of Emerson's gifts.
" Friend and aider of those who would live in the
spirit," unconquerable optimist—up to the beautiful
ending. It is significant of Arnold's deep seriousness that he wished to be remembered chiefly by
this volume—this volume so full of that particular
moral judgment which he brought to bear on all
individual and national life. Arnold's literary work
has been treated here separately. It will be found
one with all his work.

WRITINGS ON SOCIETY AND POLITICS

Bibliography

1859.   " England and the Italian Question."   A pamphlet.

1861.   " Democracy," reprinted with this title in " Mixed Essays," originally the Introduction to " The Popular Education of France," etc.   1861.

1866.   " My Countrymen," *The Cornhill Magazine*, February.   "An Explanation," a letter to the *Pall Mall Gazette*, March 20th, reprinted in " Friendship's Garland," 1871.   Letters to the *Pall Mall Gazette*, Nos. 1-5 in " Friendship's Garland," July 21st, August 4th, 7th and 15th, November 8th.

1867.   Letters to the *Pall Mall Gazette*, Nos. 6 and 7 in " Friendship's Garland," April 20th and 22nd. "Culture and its Enemies," *The Cornhill Magazine*, July, reprinted in " Culture and Anarchy."

1868.   " Anarchy and Authority.·' Five articles in *The Cornhill Magazine*, January, February, June, July, August, reprinted in " Culture and Anarchy."

1869.   Letter to the *Pall Mall Gazette*, June 8th, Letter eight, in " Friendship's Garland."

1870.   Letters to the *Pall Mall Gazette*, Nos. 9-12 in " Friendship's Garland," August 9th, November 21st, 25th, 29th.

1878. " Equality." *The Fortnightly Review*, ⎫ Reprinted in
      March. " Irish Catholicism and   ⎪ " *Mixed*
      British Liberalism, ' *The Fort-* ⎬ *Essays.*"
      nightly Review, July.   ⎭

1879. " Ecce Convertimur ad Gentes." *The* ⎫
      Fortnightly Review, February.   ⎪

1880. " The Future of Liberalism." *The* ⎪
      Nineteenth Century, July.   ⎪ Reprinted in

1881. " The Incompatibles." *The Nine-* ⎬ " *Irish*
      teenth Century, Part I, April, Part ⎪ *Essays.*"
      II, June. " Edmund Burke's ⎪
      Letters, Speeches and Tracts on ⎪
      Irish Affairs," with an Intro- ⎪
      duction.   ⎭

1882. " A Word about America," *Nineteenth Century*.

1885. " A Word more about America," February, *Nineteenth Century*.

1886. " The Nadir of Liberalism," *Nineteenth Century*, May. Letters to the *Times*. " The Political Crisis," May 22nd. " After the Elections," August 6th.

1887. " The Zenith of Conservatism." *The Nineteenth Century*, January. " Up to Easter," *The Nineteenth Century*, May. " From Easter to August," *The Nineteenth Century*, September.

1888. " Disestablishment in Wales." *The National Review*, March.

IT is evident from the order in which Arnold's writings appeared that his mind was occupied specially through distinct periods with some special subject or groups of subjects. Then, having dealt with them and " having finished " with them, as he used to say, he passed on, generally by a natural development, to another subject. We have seen already that by far the largest part of his poetry—the whole, indeed, with the exception of " Merope," " Balder Dead," " Thyrsis," and one or two other poems—was issued by 1853. Let us note that he had produced nothing else. In 1857 he was appointed to the Chair of Poetry at Oxford for a period of five years, and again for five years. During this time, that is 1857-1867, the larger part of his literary criticism was done, comprising " On Translating Homer," the First Series of " Essays in Criticism," " On the Study of Celtic Literature." This body of work, produced apparently with such spontaneity and sureness, at once established the value of Arnold's literary judgments. In the same period, and side by side with this work of literary criticism, he published also his Reports on the Educational Systems of Holland, Switzerland, France and Germany, and these we have already considered.

The materials for these Reports had been gathered during his tour in 1859 as Foreign Assistant Commissioner of the Commission to report on the systems of elementary education ; and in 1865 on his tour to France, Germany, Italy and Switzerland as Commissioner of the Middle Class Schools Inquiry Commission to enquire into the secondary education of the Continent. These two Commissions gave Arnold unique facilities for a close and detailed observation of Continental society. It was probably due to Dr. Arnold that the insularity so characteristic of Englishmen generally was never true of Dr. Arnold's son. Dr. Arnold's travelling journals, collected at the end of Dean Stanley's Life, are the best witness to the large experience with which he surrounded his children. Matthew was abroad with him in France in 1837 and again in 1841. He was in Belgium in 1854, in Switzerland 1858, in Belgium again in 1860 and on extended tours during 1859 and 1865.

This contact with French and German society had an important influence upon Arnold himself, which we shall consider later. For the present the point to note is, that it induced in Arnold the comparative study of European societies, and gave him that detached point of view from which with his faculty of direct, intuitive perception he could detect and mark the failings of his countrymen. It enabled him, in short, to produce his writing on Social Criticism. In reference to this, however, we must note that Arnold in the period between the two tours as Commissioner, 1859 and 1865, had a strong and constant intention to write more poetry. On 15th August, 1861, he wrote to his mother :

" I must finish off for the present my critical writings between this and forty (he was nearly 39), and give the next ten years earnestly to poetry. It is my last chance. It is not a bad ten years of one's life for poetry, if one resolutely uses it, but it is a time in which, if one does not use it, one dries up and becomes prosaic altogether."

I do not think Arnold would have turned at this time in the direction of Social Criticism, if it had not been for the appointment of 1865 from the Middle Class Schools Inquiry Commission. That he would have turned to Social Criticism at some time is probable, and at this time, in 1863, just before his appointment on the Middle Class Schools Inquiry Commission 1865, he published his articles on " A French Eton," based upon materials which he had gathered on the 1859 Commission. " A French Eton " shows and develops still further the ideas contained in the article "Democracy," which we have considered in Arnold's educational work. But it should be noted here in its origin from the continental Commission and also as showing all the ideas which later came into " Culture and Anarchy." The ideas were in Arnold's mind in 1861 in " Democracy," and in 1863 in " A French Eton." But at times other voices were calling him. In a letter to Mr. (afterwards Sir) M. E. Grant-Duff, M.P., on 24th May, 1864, he writes :

" One is from time to time seized and irresistibly carried along by a temptation to treat political, or religious, or social matters directly, but after yielding to such temptation I always feel myself recoiling again, and disposed to touch them only so far as they can be touched through poetry."

It has been said in an earlier chapter that the main part of Arnold's poetry had been published by 1854, that is, before he was 33 (Note : " Poems by Matthew Arnold," Second Series, 1855, was printed by December, 1854). So far the creative tendency in his mind had been uppermost, and had produced a body of poetry not indeed large, but of perfect workmanship. The appointment to the Oxford Chair of Poetry then comes to him in 1857, and from this time while the critical faculty in him seems to have come more and more into play, the creative faculty, working in the direction of poetry, almost ceased. It is true that again and again we see Arnold reserving a place in his plans for more poetry, but possibly the duties of his office and certainly the tendency of his genius drew him into the sphere of literary criticism. His work in this sphere we considered in the last chapter. At present we have to note that the same insight and taste which working, on literary materials, had shaped the first " Essays in Criticism " now turned to observe the social and political condition of English life. One cannot trace in

Arnold the process of the unfolding of the critical faculty. A greater skill and ease, an increasing mastery and extension, in a word, development, of these Arnold apparently had none, for the critical gift appears in him immediately at a mature and sustained level.

Between 1861 and 1867, as has been said previously, " Essays in Criticism," " On Translating Homer," and " Celtic Literature," were published. In April, 1865, he started on the tour in connection with Continental Secondary Education, and was away from England, with the exception of a week at Easter, until the following November. During that time he visited France, Italy, Germany, Austria and Switzerland. Arnold was thus brought again into contact with the societies of the Continent, and the circumstances of his tour gave him the opportunity of a perpendicular view of each of them. As a man of letters of eminence he had access to the higher classes of Paris and Berlin ; as the representative of a Government Commission he had immediate entrance into the official circles of Continental societies, which represented perhaps a larger area of society than in England ; as a Commissioner on Education he saw through the schools into the heart of the societies which created them. In Paris he saw Guizot, Sainte-Beuve and Schérer, the *Revue des Deux Mondes* set, as he calls them, and the *Journal des Débats* set.

He visited Princess Mathilde ; and through the embassies and his letters of introduction appears to have seen much of the official classes. His letters at this time begin to show his critical observation of the national characteristics of the Continent. Of the Italians, for instance, he wrote :

> " The Piedmontese is the only virile element—he is like a country Frenchman—but he is still leaven to leaven the whole lump. And the whole lump want backbone, serious energy, and power of honest work, to a degree that makes one impatient. I am tempted to take the Professors I see in the schools by the collar, and hold them down to their work for five or six hours a day—so angry do I get at their shirking and inefficiency. They have all a certain refinement which they call civilisation, but a nation is really civilised by acquiring the qualities it by nature is wanting in ; and the Italians are no more civilised by virtue of their refinement alone, than we are civilised by virtue of our energy alone."

Arnold thus being brought into contact with the Continental societies in a way that gave him exceptional opportunities for a wide and accurate knowledge, was led naturally to comparison of these with the condition of society in our own land. We may turn aside here to note also that Arnold's circumstances in this country gave him special opportunities of observing different classes of society. His father's position as Headmaster of Rugby brought him into contact with the upper class. Arnold himself had been Lord Lansdowne's Private Secretary. He married the daughter of Mr Justice Wightman. His letters are full of references to visits to, and friendships with many of the best known names of the aristocracy, the Russells, Peels and Aclands. But his professional work gave him even a closer acquaintance with the middle class. For 35 years he worked in the towns near London, and consequently saw many different homes. As Inspector, during many years, of schools connected with both the Church of England and with Dissent, he was necessarily the recipient of the hospitality of the managers. He had known what it was to be prayed for by name and to have his faults gently hinted at in the family devotions. ("Thomas and Matthew Arnold," Sir Joshua Fitch, p. 224.)

He returned to England from the Middle Class Schools Inquiry Commission tour in November, 1865. There appeared early in 1866, "My Countrymen," in the *Cornhill*. That it was written as a result of his continental visit is evident :

"... having lately had occasion to travel on the Continent for many months, during which I was thrown in company with a great variety of people, I remembered what Burns says of the profitableness of trying to see ourselves as others see us, and I kept on the watch for anything to confirm or contradict my old notion, in which, without absolutely giving it up, I had begun certainly to be much shaken and staggered."

Arnold regarded this article as a careful and important utterance, and shows in one of his letters considerable interest in its reception. The article was afterwards published in *Friendship's Garland*, where it is humorously and ingeniously brought into the framework of the book. It should be read first since it sets out formally the opinions which the letters in *Friendship's Garland* wittily illustrate.

The target of the article is the fact expressed in the statement " the heart of the English nation is its middle class." Mr. Miall, Mr. Bazley, *The Daily Telegraph*, *The Daily News* and *The Morning Star*, are all brought in to illustrate this. Criticism by infinitesimals it may be, but there is something infinitely amusing in Arnold's selection of some unfortunate expression of his victim which he takes up alone and unsupported, turning it mercilessly round and round apparently as a fair and representative utterance, until under this treatment it comes to look like concentrated foolishness. Mr. Bazley (now Sir Thomas Bazley, Bart., Matthew Arnold reminds us in a note), the member for Manchester, the middle class metropolis, makes a speech in which he expresses surprise at the clamour raised for better middle-class education.

The *Daily Telegraph*, commenting on it, says that
" he talked to his constituents as Manchester people
like to be talked to, in the language of clear, manly
intelligence, which penetrates through sophisms,
ignores commonplaces and gives to conventional
illusions their true value. Arnold, as we have
said, had just returned from the Continent and knew
well how the middle class education of England
compared with that of the Continent, and saw its
results in the blind pride of that section of his
countrymen. When, therefore, an M.P., applauded
by the daily press, flatters them and their education,
Arnold unflinchingly tells them the truth as he
sees it. He takes the foreign policy of England
under a middle class government, that of Lord
Palmerston, and compares it with the foreign
policy, under the government of an aristocracy,
of the Duke of Wellington. In 1865 it
is the aristocracy that administers as a weak
extreme naturally must, with a nervous attention to the wishes of the strong middle
part :

> " Rash engagement, intemperate threatening, un-
> dignified retreat, ill-timed cordiality, are not the faults
> of an aristocracy by nature in such concerns prudent,
> reticent, dignified, sensitive on the point of honour ;
> they are rather the faults of a rich middle class, testy,
> absolute, ill-acquainted with foreign matters, a little
> ignoble, very dull to perceive when it is making itself
> ridiculous."

It was the middle class which made the American war, which abused Germany in the dispute with Denmark, which taunted Germany with chastisement by France, which slighted the American Federals. England is neglected on the Continent. There they know that no serious effort at government exists in England. The dozen men at the head of affairs wait to see how the British Philistine will act—" a sitting in devout expectation to see how the cat will jump," as in a letter in " Friendship's Garland " he phrases it.

" Was Russia, at a critical moment, to lose precious time waiting for the chance medley of accidents, intrigues, hot and cold fits, stock-jobbing, newspaper articles, conversations on the railway, conversations on the omnibus, out of which grows the foreign policy of a self-governing people, when that self is the British Philistine ? "

What is the result of this ?

" Why, taking Lord Palmerston's career from 1830 (when he first became Foreign Secretary) to his death, there cannot be a shadow of doubt, for anyone with eyes and ears in his head, that he found England the first Power in the world's estimation, and that he leaves her the third after France and the United States."

Compare with this, England under the government of an aristocracy, the Napoleonic period :

" They had a vigorous lower class, a vigorous middle class, and a vigorous aristocracy. The lower class worked and fought, the middle class found the money, and the aristocracy wielded the whole. This aristocracy was high-spirited, reticent, firm, despising frothy declamation. It had all the qualities useful for its task and time ; Lord Grenville's words, as early as 1793, ' England will never consent that France shall arrogate the power of annulling at her pleasure, and under the pretence of a pretended natural right, the political system of Europe' —these few words with their lofty strength, contain, as one may say, the prophecy of future success ; you hear the very voice of an aristocracy standing on sure ground, and with the stars in its favour. Well, you succeeded, and in 1815, after Waterloo, you were the first power in Europe."—(" My Country-men.")

Keeping to this representative article on " My Countrymen," we have seen Arnold's criticism of English foreign policy under middle class Government. He goes on to the praised performances of the great middle class in home affairs, taking a speech of Mr. Lowe, (Lord Sherbrooke), as an illustrative eulogy. In answer to this he shows how well the aristocracy in their time and place performed the work which the development of society had laid upon them.

" Their talents were for other times and tasks ; for curbing the power of the Crown, when other classes were too inconsiderable to do it ; for managing (if one com-pares them with other aristocracies), their affairs and their dependants with vigour, prudence, and moderation, during the feudal and patriarchal stage of society ; for wielding the force of their country against foreign powers with energy, firmness and dignity."

Then with the expansions of human life came the hour of the middle class, for the government of the many :

" Have you succeeded, are you succeeding, in this hour of the many, as your aristocracy succeeded in the hour of the few ? . . . What do you make of the mass of your society, of its vast middle and lower portion ? . . . Without insisting too much on the stories of misery and degradation which are perpetually reaching us, we will say that no one can mix with a great crowd in your country, no one can walk with his eyes and ears open through the poor quarters of your large towns, and not feel that your common people, as it meets one's eyes, is at present more raw, to say the very least, less enviable—looking, further removed from civilised and humane life, than the common people almost anywhere."

This is a strain in which Arnold might well have written more often than he did. The critical faculty requires material to work upon, and no doubt such a finely wrought, critical mind as was Arnold's is better fitted for the delicate piercing of weak spots than the heavy artillery which alone is effective upon some social evils. No one will want the subtle raillery of " Friendship's Garland " exchanged for, say, the tones of a Trade Union Secretary, yet Arnold would to a great extent have disarmed prejudice, would even have established his influence in another region, and would at the same time

L

have spoken what he truly felt, if the " armies of the homeless and the unfed," as he put it in a sonnet, had in his attacks upon errors in society more often received his eminent help.

We have now come in " My Countrymen " to the central voice of Arnold's critical spirit, his judgment of the social condition of the middle class itself, its education, its business, its pleasure, its religion, its daily life. Beginning with this article Arnold for five years made the middle class the chief object of his satire and fun and banter and mockery and plain speaking. If we take the number of men who are brought into service for quotation ; the papers, the politicians, all the ecclesiastics and self-condemned figures that Arnold passes before us ; and note the humorous dialogues, the scenic attitudes, the unfortunate utterances, the mock humility, all directed with a careful, critical aim, whether we admit its impartiality or not, we shall say that there is nothing in English literature comparable to it for fresh and select diction and for brilliance and fertility of idea.

The conclusion of " My Countrymen " deals with the middle class want of intelligence. " Your intellect is at this moment to an almost unexampled degree without influence on the intellect of Europe." France knows its own ideas and believes in them ; America, "blindly as they seem following in general the star of their god, Buncombe," yet has its strong

democratic feeling firmly fixed on the future, and
is shaping its course accordingly. They all read our
best books, the books which here already are still
only read by a few. But we, with our middle class,
with a great start in freedom and wealth, have intelligence only for industry and for doing a roaring trade.

> " Your middle class man thinks it the highest pitch of
> development and civilisation when his letters are carried
> twelve times a day from Islington to Camberwell, and
> from Camberwell to Islington, and if railway trains run
> to and fro between them every quarter of an hour. He
> thinks it is nothing that the trains only carry him from
> an illiberal dismal life at Islington, to an illiberal dismal
> life at Camberwell, and the letters only tell him that such
> is the life there. A Swiss burgher takes heavens knows
> how many hours to go from Berne to Geneva, and his
> trains are very few : this is an extreme on the other
> side ; but compare the life the Swiss burgher finds or
> leaves at Berne or Geneva with the life of the middle
> class in your English town."—(" Friendship's Garland,"
> 146-147.)

" My Countrymen " attracted a good deal of
interest, specially among Arnold's friends, and
perhaps a good deal of resentment from others.
One letter in criticism of this article, signed
" Horace " but written, as Arnold says, " by a
woman I know something of in Paris, a half Russian,
half English woman who married a Frenchman,"
was answered by him in the *Pall Mall Gazette*,
19th March 1866. It is interesting—every line in

" Friendship's Garland " is interesting—specially for the humorous picture which Arnold draws of himself " shivering in my garret, listening nervously to the voices of indignant Philistines asking the way to Grub Street." The volume entitled " Friendship's Garland " consists of the article, " My Countrymen," and its sequel, " A Courteous Explanation," together with twelve letters and a dedicatory letter.

These twelve letters were contributed to the " *Pall Mall Gazette*," between 19th July 1866 and 26th November 1870, and formed the bulk of the book. Arminius is a Prussian character represented to be an acquaintance of Arnold. He is described as visiting England, and in various conversations and letters criticises what he sees of the English people. He went at last to the Franco-Prussian war and died at the siege of Paris. To him, Matthew Arnold, following the motto " manibus date lilia plenis," lovingly makes this memorial, " Friendship's Garland : being the conversations, letters, and opinions of the late Arminius, Baron von Thunder-Ten-Tronckh. Collected and edited, with a dedicatory letter to Adolescens Leo Esq., of *The Daily Telegraph*." The humour is extremely subtle and allusive. Arminius is, of course, the voice of Arnold's own criticisms, while Arnold himself is the mock representative and advocate of his countrymen.

It is easy to see how under this arrangement of characters Arnold's inventiveness and fun produce some delightful satire. Being letters to the *Pall Mall Gazette*, they contain many allusions to contemporary occurrences and personalities, but the critical thrusts beneath the banter and the inimitable mockery will make them a classic in the lighter critical literature—*will* make them, I say, for " Friendship's Garland " is not yet known. We are shown Mr. Hepworth Dixon, " as I passed down Regent Street yesterday and saw in a shop window, in the frontispiece to one of Mr. Hepworth Dixon's numerous but well-merited editions, the manly and animated features of the author of the immortal ' Guide to Mormonism,' I could not help exclaiming with pride, I too am an author ; " Mr. G. A. Sala ; (" I told Sala what had happened, ' The old story,' " says Sala, " life a dream, take a glass of brandy ") ; Lord Elcho (everybody knows Lord Elcho's appearance and how admirably he looks the part of our governing classes, to my mind, indeed, the mere cock of his lordship's hat is one of the finest and most aristocratic things we have). So of course I pointed Lord Elcho out to Arminius. Arminius eyed him with a Jacobinical sort of smile, and then, " Cedar of Lebanon which God has not yet broken ! " Mr. Frederic Harrison, in full evening costume, furbishing up a guillotine. Dr. Russell of *The Times* preparing to mount his war-horse. You know the sort of thing—he has described it himself over and over again. Bismarck at his horse head, the Crown Prince holding his stirrup, and the old King of Prussia hoisting Russell into the saddle, these are unforgettable vignettes. Arnold defends his countrymen from Arminius' aspersions, and expresses the current pride in the great commercial achievements of British civilisation ; he is, in short, the average, self-satisfied, practical Englishman, proud of his great industrial life, satisfied with education, obedient to the great daily press, complacent in his accumulating wealth, disregarding beauty, blind to the necessity for the application of intelligence to private and public conduct, ignorant of the judgment of the outside world, all self-bound in his material pursuits and considerations. Against these Arminius launches his plain strong condemnations, always rebuked by Arnold for his strong language and his want of respect for good taste. He urges the Englishman to tell his countrymen that they should leave clap-trap and cultivate " Geist," intelligence, the idea of a science governing every department of human activity. By clap-trap he means the Press, which he hits with light shafts of satire again and again. (" I take the *Star* for wisdom and charity, and the *Telegraph* for taste and style.")

One letter expounds Stein's reforms in Prussian

land tenure ; another introduces the subject of
Compulsory Education. The artillery is then
turned upon the kind of men who administer
justice as magistrates. Arnold selects three, Vis-
count Lumpington, Rev. Esau Hittall, and Bottles
Esquire, who happen to be trying a poacher,
poor Zephaniah Diggs. The character-sketches
of the three are merciless. Their education is
treated from the point of view of its value as a preparation for the intelligent administration of justice.
Arnold's view is that education should be a bar
or condition, between the man and what he aims at !
The satirical, mocking treatment of personalities such
as these was always in Arnold's inimitable manner.
It would be difficult to equal in humour the last
glimpse of Lord Lumpington : " Never mind,
Arminius, said I, soothingly, run after Lumpington and ask him the square root of thirty-six."
The next letter, supposed to be by Leo, the young
lion of *The Daily Telegraph*, is a hit at the Liberal
party for its leaning towards the proposed legalisation
of marriage with a deceased wife's sister. Arminius'
description of Macaulayese and the introduction
of the " forgotten word, delicacy " in connection
with Mr. Sala are the two good points. By this
time the Franco-Prussian war had broken out, and
Arnold uses this to send Arminius off to the Prussian
war, addressing as he goes a " Disrespectful Farewell
to our People and Institutions." Arminius says

that our foreign policy is directed by a weak aristocracy administered on behalf of the middle class. The letter entitled " Life's a Dream " is exquisitely humorous, and cannot possibly be condensed.

" Friendship's Garland," being chiefly letters to the *Pall Mall Gazette*, is in the lighter journalistic strain, but a strain which Arnold worked brilliantly. The letters and the article " My Countrymen " cover a period of five years, from the end of 1865 to the end of 1870, but they have been brought into a curious unity by the editing of them as a memorial of the unfortunate Prussian. The skilful conduct of the conversations, in which Arnold's criticisms of English life are put into the blunt expressions of a foreigner, the general banter, the mock humility, make most delightful reading. The charges brought against the character of English politics and society were perfectly serious and just. It is noticeable that while the first edition of " Friendship's Garland " was published in 1871, the second edition did not appear until 1897, but it did appear significantly then.

Between the seventh and eighth letters in " Friendship's Garland " there is an interval of over two years, that is from 21st April 1867, to 8th June 1869. Arnold explains it by saying that a rupture between himself and Arminius had occurred, and that Arnold had been abandoned for Mr. Frederic Harrison. As a matter of fact, in that interval Arnold makes his greatest contribution to Social Criticism, the several articles which compose " Culture and Anarchy." It is possible that he was induced by the expressions of his friends and critics to gather his views upon the condition of English society and his suggestions for reform into a compact body. So far they had been uttered here and there, but perhaps lacked effectiveness through being unconnected with a body of opinions moving on definite principles to a clearly defined end. Mr. Frederic Harrison had said, " We seek vainly in Mr. Arnold a system of philosophy with principles coherent, inter-dependent, subordinate, and derivative." Matthew Arnold made fun of this sentence, but it had effect on him. At any rate, in editing " Friendship's Garland," when he comes to the interval mentioned above, the interval when " Culture and Anarchy " was produced, he quotes Mr. Frederic Harrison's sentence.

The articles composing " Culture and Anarchy " were published in the *Cornhill Magazine* between July 1867, and February 1868. Arnold worked at the preface in the latter part of 1868, and the completed book was published in February 1869. He was then living at Harrow and wrote on his birthday a letter to his mother which shows a deep inwardness of character. The death during the year of his two little boys, Basil and Tom, and the fact that he had reached to within a year of his father's age at death, would seem to have affected him considerably and seriously. He speaks of the " settlement " of his thought. " Culture and Anarchy " is an illustration of this. It indicates a definite point of view ; the possession of certain positive principles, which regulated his outlook on social affairs, and guided him in the advocacy of remedies for what he considered to be the defects of our civilisation. Arnold with modesty perhaps half-mocking, disclaimed any attempt at a system, and always represented himself as the plain man of the street, speaking common sense. Nevertheless, he did in his own unique way set forth a positive theory of social aims. He did so in " Culture and Anarchy." This is probably what he meant by the " settlement of his own thought."

Arnold gives an interesting account in the same letter of his habits of work at this time.

" I am up at six and work at the preface to my ' Culture and Anarchy,' essays, work again at this and read between breakfast and luncheon, play racquets and walk between luncheon and four, from four to seven look over my 25 papers, and then after dinner write my letters and read a little."

" Culture and Anarchy " is a well known book. Its phrases have passed into the language of literature and of the Press, and are familiar to many people who do not know their original connection. The best known, " Sweetness and Light," was Dean Swift's phrase, but it was Arnold's genius which selected and brought it to life, and used it persistently until it had fixed itself in current use. The " Philistines", and Culture as "the best that has been thought and said," " Hebraism and Hellenism " are all the phrases of " Culture and Anarchy." The title at first sight is a curious combination, but it is explained by the origin of the book. The original article in the *Cornhill* was " Culture and its Enemies," and the two later ones, " Anarchy and Authority." What induced Arnold to deal with this subject ? We have seen that he was probably feeling the necessity of stating his attitude, not only as a critic of social affairs, but also as a positive constructive thinker. The particular direction of his thought was determined by the event just then happening. The articles referred to above were published in July and December, 1867, a year of great social and political unrest. The country was heaving with excitement at the Reform Bill introduced by Lord John Russell and Mr. Gladstone in 1866. The Bill had been defeated and Lord Derby had formed a new ministry with Mr. Disraeli.

But the people were determined to show their will in favour of the Reform Bill, and a furious agitation ran through all the country. Everywhere new political associations were formed. Meetings were held, and especially a great demonstration was announced for Hyde Park on 23rd July. The Home Secretary, Mr. Walpole, unwisely prohibited it. The leaders of the meeting being refused admittance to the Park then went to Trafalgar Square and there held an orderly meeting. The crowd however which remained at the Park soon became unruly, and finally tore down the railings for half a mile. All through the night there was wild excitement, and considerable damage was done to the Park. Rumours of revolt and quite an outbreak of anarchy spread through London, causing a great deal of uneasiness. Mr. Walpole appears to have acted very weakly in the matter, at first injudicially prohibiting the meeting and then giving way when confronted by the leaders of the movement.

The agitation for Reform was continued through the winter of 1866, by public demonstrations in which the new Trade Unions took a prominent part. In the following year, 1867, a meeting was announced for 6th May, in Hyde Park. Again the Government prohibited it but the meeting was held, amid great expectation and excitement. During the same period a series of attacks upon life and property, known as the Sheffield outrages, had been perpetrated in that town. Workmen suspected by the local trade unions were victims of attacks upon themselves and their houses. Crime after crime was committed in this way, till at last, in 1867, a Commission was appointed to enquire into their causes. An elaborate secret organisation for punishing offences against the laws of certain trade unions was discovered, and several other towns were found to be nearly as bad as Sheffield.

Fenianism, too, at this time was rampant. Canada was actually invaded by the Fenian army on 31st May 1866. In England a plan was formed to seize Chester Castle in February 1867. In May 1867, Colonel Burke was sentenced to death, but a great outburst of national feeling saved his life. Then a rescue of Fenian prisoners in Manchester was attempted, in which a policeman was killed. In December the trouble entered London, when a barrel of gunpowder was placed by Fenians against the House of Detention in Clerkenwell with the object of releasing two Fenian prisoners. The agitation for Reform, the secret terrorising, and the wide-spread Fenianism undoubtedly revealed a bad state of society. Law and order seemed to be threatened on every side. What perhaps emphasized the feeling of instability was the fact that the causes of this discontent were real, and needed to be removed before equilibrium and progress could be secured.

Doubtless these things were in Arnold's mind when " Anarchy and Authority " and " Culture and its Enemies " were written—written as we have seen, between July 1867 and 1868, just when the country was agitated by these events.   Arnold did not like the Hyde Park rioting, nor the weak attitude of the authorities towards it.

> " . . . this and that man, and this and that body of men, all over the country are beginning to assert and put in practice an Englishman's right to do what he likes, meet where he likes, enter where he likes, hoot as he likes, threaten as he likes, smash as he likes. All this, I say, tends to anarchy."—(" Culture and Anarchy," p. 37.)

Arnold saw, however, that English society was passing through a revolution, and makes frequent references to the troubled state of social life.   It is quite clear that he intended in " Culture and Anarchy " to state his ideal of culture as a preventive against the existing unrest and fermentation.

Yet it would not be correct to assume that the contemporary state of society was the chief cause of " Culture and Anarchy."   The existing disorder was the occasion of its appearance, but in a perfectly composed and well ordered period Matthew Arnold would have set forth the same ideals of individual development and social aims. Those ideals were rooted in his nature ; they were the laws of his own life, and that he should try to exhibit them attractively to his fellow men was inevitable.   He saw the state of feeling about him, the development of anarchic forces, the disappearance of civilising influences, and so proposed as a counteracting force his own individual and personal ideal of life. Arnold was practical, but he was not a man of action. In his humorous manner he wrote often of his concern only with the plain, commonplace view of things, his concern only with doing; yet his influence will always be that of a man of thought rather than that of a man of action ; certainly dealing with action, but from the standpoint of a thinker and a critic. Unfortunate it will be if Arnold's admirers regard " Culture and Anarchy " as a really serious and workable contribution to social reform. To have proposed Culture—the knowing the best that has been thought and said—as a preventive against such amenities as Fenianism, Sheffield outrages, and Hyde Park rioting, would surely be pills for earthquakes. We had better treat it as the expression of his own personal ideal of life. Were it realised, indeed, the one and the other of these social diseases would be impossible.

Let us now state the substance of " Culture and Anarchy." It is in the first place an analysis of English society. In the second place it sets forth certain ideals of social life. Arnold divides English society into three classes : the Aristocracy, the Middle Class, and the Lower Class ; or, as he calls them respectively, Barbarians, Philistines and Populace. The Barbarians, he says, reinvigorated and renewed worn-out Europe : they brought staunch individualism, a passion for doing as one likes, the love of field sports, the care of the body, and chivalry.   Our aristocracy in England has exterior culture.   It insists on the right of personal liberty : it has good looks and complexion, ease and politeness, distinguished manners, high spirits ; and so, by the possession of these qualities, they may be called Barbarians.   Their failings are a want of light, of ideas, they are "children of the established fact," inaccessible to ideas ; their culture is entirely exterior.   (We have followed closely Arnold's own phrases.)

To illustrate the qualities of the aristocracy, Arnold selects as the happy mean a " well-known lord," and as their excess a well-known baronet. But for a really humorous picture of the true Barbarian we must go to "Friendship's Garland " and the Lord Lumpington already mentioned.   We see Lumpington at school, nourished on the " grand old fortifying classical curriculum " ; spending his time in hunting, getting his degree by three weeks' cramming under a famous coach for fast men.   We see him a magistrate, made a magistrate by the Lumpington estate, not after any educational preparation for the office.   This gives rise to the humorous incident in which Arminius hits off the situation, and Arnold, summing up in a word the condition of the aristocracy, says that they are materialised. In other places he showed that we had outgrown them. They are materialised, he said in 1879, because of our system of landed inheritance, which secures not the equal division of property among a man's children, but the passing of the land to the eldest child. Consequently a system of great landed estates ministers to mere pleasure and indulgence. When a number of centres of strong government was needed the system worked well : but now it tends to materialise the owners.

For an epoch of concentration, or as we might better say, of consolidation, when a firm administration of the existing system is necessary for the settling and the strengthening of its parts, an aristocracy is eminently fitted. But for an epoch of expansion, when new ideas, new interests and new alterations of the proportion of political power disturb the status quo and demand the application of intelligence in order to secure a new equilibrium for such a time, an aristocracy is not fitted. For an epoch of concentration energy is wanted, and that the aristocracy has. But for an epoch of expansion ideas are wanted, and ideas the aristocracy has not. It has a bent for preserving the thing that is : but for the harmonising of new interests it has no gift. With the other end of the social scale Arnold scarcely dealt. There are few references to the poorer portion of our society : and

M

with the powerful humanitarian forces guiding us to-day we can well wish that both in matter and in manner Arnold had shown more sympathy and insight on this subject. He compares the English masses with the French to the disadvantage of the former, who, he says, not being disciplined by conscription, have not the idea of public duty as superior to the individual will, which the French masses have. He goes even further and suggests a want of courage among workmen, illustrating it from the men of the district of Derby during the Crimean war.

The Hyde Park riots were fresh in the public mind at the time Arnold was writing, and the roughness and violence shown he frequently selects in order to illustrate the working man's particular form of vice, doing as one likes.

> " But that vast portion, lastly, of the working class which, raw and half-developed, has long lain half hidden amidst its poverty and squalor, and is now issuing from its hiding-place to assert an Englishman's heaven-born privilege of doing as he likes, and is beginning to perplex us by marching where it likes, meeting where it likes, bawling what it likes, breaking what it likes, to this vast residuum we may with great propriety give the name of Populace."—(" Culture and Anarchy," 66.)

As in the case of the aristocratic class, Arnold selects examples of what he calls the excess, the happy mean, and the defect of the working class.

For the excess he takes Mr. Bradlaugh, whom Arnold charges with intemperate talk. To illustrate the defects of the working class he selects " my poor old poaching friend Zephaniah Diggs, who between his hare-snaring and his gin-drinking has got his powers of sympathy quite dulled and his powers of action in any great movement of his class hopelessly impaired." For the happy mean he selects Mr. Odger, "with whom there is manifestly, with all his good points, some insufficiency of light."

One must regret Arnold's lack of sympathy in his treatment of the Populace. For him the full stream had not risen, as it has for us, which carries us to a nearer view of the social causes of a great deal of poverty, which carries us in a great movement of sympathy to a sounder political economy. Probably the opportunity of satire was irresistible to Arnold. In reality he saw clearly and rightly the defects and the black spots on our social life. We shall see later how in his positive teaching he insisted on the need of an expansion of culture which would include the whole social body. Further, that his satirical attacks do not fairly show his deeper feelings towards the working class may be seen from the Sonnet to a Republican Friend, 1848 :

> " If sadness at the long heart-wasting show
> Wherein earth's great ones are disquieted ;
> If thoughts, not idle, while before me flow
> The armies of the homeless and unfed—

If these are yours, if this is what you are,
Then am I yours, and what you feel I share."

Arnold distinguished between the lower and the higher working class. The lower he called the Populace, the higher he treated as belonging to the middle class, because by means of trade unions it asserted its own distinct class self, and because it had the aims of the middle class. At a later time Arnold suddenly and somewhat curiously addressed himself to this upper portion of the working class. In January 1879, he delivered an address to the Working Men's College at Ipswich, at the time the largest of the kind in England, which was published afterwards in the *Fortnightly Review* of 1879, under the title, shall we say appropriately in Latin, " Ecce Convertimur ad Gentes." This article has been referred to already as showing the materialising effect upon the aristocracy of our system of landed inheritance. He argued that three things were necessary to the progress of our civilisation. First, a reduction of those immense inequalities of conditions and property of which our land system is the base. Second, a genuine municipal system. Third, public schools for the middle classes. But the noticeable thing is the frank way in which he appeals to the working class.

" For twenty years I have been vainly urging this upon the middle class themselves. Now I urge it upon you."

We come now to what was the loudest note in Arnold's social criticism. Up to the end of his life he waged a ceaseless war upon the middle class, Philistines as he called them. His criticisms of the upper class and of the lower class are light and genial compared to the fire which he opened upon the Philistines from every quarter and on every occasion. The wittiest, the most brilliant and caustic, the most penetrating and humorous of his writings were directed against them. The individual characters whom he placed in print, the isolated incidents and extracts, were all selected with an unerring eye for the ugly and the ill-balanced. The main feature of Arnold's Social Criticism is this incessant attack upon the pleasures, occupations, interests, education and politics of the middle class.

He called them Philistines ; and Philistine he tells us in an essay upon Heinrich Heine was derived from a German word Philister, equivalent to the French épicier.

"Efforts have been made to obtain in English some term equivalent to Philister or épicier; Mr. Carlyle has made several such efforts : ' respectability with its thousand gigs,' he says ; well, the occupant of every one of these gigs is, Mr. Carlyle means, a Philistine. However, the word respectable is far too valuable a word to be thus perverted from its proper meaning ; if the English are ever to have a word for the thing we are speaking of—and so prodigious are the changes which the modern spirit is introducing, that even we English shall perhaps one day come to want such a word—I think we had better take the term Philistine itself."—(p. 163.)

It does not appear to everyone entirely clear in its meaning, but it is settled in use now, and its application is perfectly well understood. What did Arnold find to praise in the middle class ? He praised the middle class energy, enterprise, self-reliance, seriousness. But on the other side he set down an overwhelming indictment. The middle class, said Arnold, has two concerns : the concern for making money and the concern for saving their souls. To illustrate this he brings in a ghastly newspaper case of a man named Smith who committed suicide, labouring " under the apprehension that he would come to poverty and that he was eternally lost." For its humour and perhaps for its unfairness this is a good example of Arnold's method of argument— argument by infinitesimals, as it has been called. The characteristics of civilisation are the love of industry and wealth, the love of things of the mind, and the love of beautiful things. Of these, said Arnold, the middle class has only the first, the love of trade and wealth, and these it does pursue with energy and success.

The attitude of the middle class to the love of things of the mind and to the love of beauty, he summarises by saying that it has a narrow range of intellect and knowledge, a stunted sense of beauty, a low standard of manners and a defective type of religion, which is a fairly comprehensive and severe charge. The delineation of middle class education in David Copperfield he entirely approved, and saw in Mr. Creakle and Salem House, immortal types of its upbringing. As an illustration of the middle class sense of beauty Arnold cites the streets of modern London, the Duke of Wellington's statue and the " black dome and grey pepper-boxes of the National Gallery " ; and another noble and elegant illustration is Cole's Truss Manufactory, on which, says Arnold, Von Thunder-Ten-Tronckh builds a profound argument for the immortality of the soul. He deals with the pleasures of the middle class in a tone entirely just. " The fineness and capacity of a man's spirit is shown by his enjoyments." What enjoyments have they ?

" The newspapers, a sort of eating and drinking which are not to our taste, a literature of books almost entirely religious or semi-religious, books utterly unreadable by an educated class anywhere, but which your middle class consumes, they say, by the hundred thousand ; and in their evenings, for a great treat, a lecture on tee-totalism or nunneries. Can any life be imagined more hideous, more dismal, more unenviable ? "—(" Friendship's Garland," p. 143.)

We come now to Arnold's treatment of Middle

Class religion, and it will be necessary to tread delicately. In a great measure he seemed to identify middle class religion with dissent, and dissent he allied with, among other things, beer-shops. His treatment of dissent will be noticed separately ; here we are concerned with his attitude toward it as the religion of the middle class. We have seen that he set down as their main interests, religion and making money. The typical man of the middle class is the Methodist grocer who illustrates these two main interests. Narrowing his view to the Methodist grocer, Arnold's estimate of middle class religion was thus not complimentary. His charge was that the religion of the ordinary man was simply an endeavour to subdue the faults of animality, and had no positive ideal of spiritual perfection. The ordinary man was satisfied with his Puritanism and his Protestantism.

" Look at the life imaged in such a newspaper as ' The Nonconformist '—a life of jealousy of the Establishment, disputes, tea meetings, openings of chapels, sermons; and then think of it as an ideal of a human life, completing itself on all sides, and aspiring with all its organs after sweetness, light and perfection!"—(" Culture and Anarchy," p. 19.)

There are constantly satirical references to the organisation of middle class religion, to its newspapers, to its meetings, to its alliance with a political party for the object of securing by their aid its favourite reforms of disestablishment and marriage with a deceased wife's sister.

Arnold thought that as a nation we were placing a wrong emphasis upon religion. At a later time he said conduct is three-fourths of life. In thus limiting the sphere of religion he came into hostile contact with the religious world. It is just here, probably, that Arnold has been most misunderstood. From the point of view of the common Christian teaching religion is the whole of life. " Religion and life are one thing or neither is anything," as Dr. George Macdonald's aphorism expresses it. By the phrase, conduct is three-fourths of life, he intended to show that matters of religion were of paramount importance yet he was taken to mean that at least over one-quarter of life we might be *free* from the restraints of religion. A better knowledge of Arnold's work would have prevented that misconception. What he actually did mean is contained in the two chapters of " Culture and Anarchy," on Hebraism and Hellenism and " Porro unum est necessarium." They contain criticism of great insight and suggestiveness and refinement. Hebraism is the name which he gave to the force which leads us to endeavour after right conduct, which lays the emphasis of life upon religion, upon strictness of conscience. The great exponent of Hebraism is the nation of Israel, and the monument of Hebraism is the

Bible. Hebraism makes the world conscious of sin, of a root of evil in our nature which must be subjugated. In the Old Testament this was to be attained by obedience to the Law; in the New Testament it is attained by devotion to Jesus Christ.

Hellenism is the free play of mind, a desire to know things rather than a desire for upright conduct. Its root idea is spontaneity of consciousness and the desire to see things as they really are. Its great exemplars are the Greeks. Arnold expresses this in the saying which he quotes, " C'est le bonheur des hommes quand ils pensent juste." The world has inclined alternately to each of these ideals.

The Pagan world with its Hellenism was unsound; it had not the basis of right conduct ; its Hellenism was incomplete, and it was broken up by Christianity, which laid emphasis upon the Hebrew view of life. Modern Europe is the outcome of this break up, and consequently is possessed by the all importance of right doing. England in particular has felt the force of Hebraism. It has felt it through Puritanism developing man on one side only. The middle class, of which Puritanism is the strongest part, thinks that it must first cultivate this strictness of conscience, and then, said Arnold, perhaps unfairly, " he even fancies it to be his right and duty, in virtue of having conquered a limited part of himself, to give unchecked swing to the remainder." The primary concern of the Puritan is to save his soul. He subdues his passions, and so far as he succeeds in this negative aim he is to be praised. But this ideal is narrow : it is not positive and spiritual, drawing him on to a harmonious development of all sides of his life. Hebraism, strictness of conscience, needs to be supplemented by Hellenism, a free play of mind, enabling us to treat the problems of our life with intelligence.

In " Culture and Anarchy " Arnold applied his notions of Hellenism to the fundamental doctrines of Puritanism. He did this more fully when he came to treat the subject of religion. In fact his work on religion was concisely the application of Hellenism to current doctrines. So far we have been considering Arnold's criticism of society in " Friendship's Garland " and " Culture and Anarchy." On the positive side, however, " Culture and Anarchy " contains a theory of the best social life. For from the diagnosis of English society which has just been stated here, and from the positive gospel of social life which Arnold preached in his unique and effective manner, we see our nation from the point of view of a just, informed and searching spirit.

We come now to consider the social ideal which Arnold set forth. He was always humorously confessing the lack of any system in his ideas, and his novel use of words and phrases apparently confirmed this : but if one looks beneath the words there is really a clear and definite conception of social aims. The true society, as Arnold conceives it, studies and pursues perfection. By perfection he means a state of progress to higher levels, by continual expansion. That expansion must have characteristics. It must be an inward condition, a dominance of the higher, better self over the lower animal self. The whole of society must move with it. It must be a general expansion. There cannot be the isolated development of a portion. So long as one part of the social body is backward, it will be a hindrance to the progress of the whole. It must be an harmonious expansion of all the powers of human nature : no line of human development may be neglected. How is this expansion to be effected ? By Culture. " Culture," he said, " has two characters. On one side it is knowledge, and is prompted by the impulse to know things, on the other side it is reform, and is prompted by the desire to make truth prevail." Culture he thus defines as the study and the pursuit of perfection. This statement of social aims is logical and clear. It provides a rational theory of reform and a justi-fication of the various interests which we feel to be praiseworthy, although we do not see so clearly how to place them in our system of life.

We feel that every man is called upon to add

his share in the work of progress. Yet when we try to press it home upon the individual, let us say, at a municipal election, we are met by the question, Why not let things go on as they are ? Why be always striving for the better ? Arnold's word expansion calls us to facts. We see that in the natural order of things, because of the conditions of lives succeeding the single life, there is a constant expansion in every direction. The preservation and the increase of life from generation to generation secures natural expansion, and the law of natural selection secures greater complexity or fulness of life, or in another word, progress. Given then this natural expansion, what is to be its character ? Arnold said it should be inward, general and harmonious. That is really a comprehensive expression for all those movements towards a higher life in the individual and in society which draw forth the energies of good men to-day. When Arnold said that expansion must be harmonious he struck at the evangelical view of religion which in the earlier days of the century taught that the greatest concern in this life was our destiny in the world to come ; struck at that view of education which limited it to the mind and did not include the body ; struck at all the influences that were robbing life of beauty and thought and freedom.

When he said that expansion must be general,

he hit powerfully the economic system which allows the existence among us of extraordinary extremes of wealth and poverty. When he said it must be inward, he warned us against the rampant materialism of his day. What is valuable in this contribution of Arnold's to the social mind is the recognition of expansion as the natural law of life : and his statement of the ideal expansion which we should endeavour to secure, and the method by which this can be done. Many will follow Arnold in his setting forth of the rational basis of Society and the ideal at which it should aim, who will not accept the method of culture which he proposes. No part of Arnold's work is more delightful than that in which he sets out the character of the perfection to be attained by culture, sweetness and light. How humorously the boisterous reformer is set over against this ideal ! How beautifully and truthfully Oxford is brought in to vindicate it ! Some friends complain that the phrases become monotonous. For instance Sir Wm. Robertson Nicoll said :

" Gradually such expressions come to be recognised as the monotonous bray of the well-accredited ass, and they have been long banished from decent society." —(*British Weekly*, 15th June, 1899.)

Certainly that is not sweetness. To bring in these phrases continually, to insist again and again upon one or two truths was the manner of Arnold, deliberately chosen and pursued, and it must be judged as a literary manner. But there are criticisms to be brought fairly against the gospel of Culture. It is so dependent on books, yet large classes of the community sharing in the general harmonious and inward expansion do so without any reliance on books. The development and the perfecting of the literary man is accomplished by the aid of books, but the artist, the scientist, and the politician do not necessarily know the best that has been thought and said. Arnold's theory of culture will fit the minds of those inclined to books, but not everyone has this taste. Many persons have not, who yet are good citizens. Their share in the expansion of society is reached by means of art or science or even entertainment. Arnold possibly conceived the limitations of this theory, for in the Rede Lecture given at Cambridge in 1882 on Literature and Science, he endeavoured to show that culture was not merely belles-lettres but included physical science. Indeed if one may prophesy from the tendency of educational methods, books seem to be of less and less importance.

Arnold's theory of social reform being mainly dependent on books, it is ineffective against the solid evils of an unequal distribution of wealth and the effects which follow : poverty, ignorance, and anarchy. For everyone who has come face to face with our lower classes, for example those in Soho or Kensal Town, even in the days of prosperity, and has seen their mode of life, their food, their housing, their clothing, their pleasures, their use of time; or who has seen them in periods of bad trade, when suppressed discontent shows itself in sullen communism, the futility of recommending culture to those who can scarcely read is ironically apparent.

More than fifty years have passed since " Culture and Anarchy " was published, and the social conditions to which it refers are altered. Consequently the present generation has small means of realising the force of Arnold's criticism of the richer, middle and poorer classes. Whether the richer class has outgrown its materialism or not, few of us will care to say. But that the middle class is less vulgar, and that culture has spread, and with it refinement, is beyond question. And that freedom and some larger participation in the better things of life have come to the poorer classes, is happily true: true because of the life and the efforts of a band of men who, working each on his own lines, applied to the social life in which they moved a criticism high and noble and fruitful.

POLITICS

In the chapter on Arnold's Social Criticism we have already considered some of his political writings in the years 1866-9. The articles and letters which compose " Culture and Anarchy " are in the list which heads Chapter V. The distinctions between his social and political work are not always maintained, but it has been more convenient to treat the writings mentioned rather as a part of his criticism of social conditions than as politics. Some parts, however, are clearly political, as for example, in " Culture and Anarchy " the chapter " Our Liberal Practitioners." Of this work in 1866-9, the main characteristic is that the social condition of the nation is the chief object of attention, politics being regarded as secondary to this. The last of this work of social criticism was the preface to " Culture and Anarchy," published in 1869. In connection with this he wrote to his mother on his birthday, December 24th :

" I am up at six and work at the preface to my ' Culture and Anarchy ' Essays."—(" Letters " Vol. I, p. 402.)

Arnold then definitely closed with social and political questions until 1878. On 28th January, 1869, he wrote Lady de Rothschild.

"Now I have done with Social and Political essays for a long time to come."—("Letters," Vol. II, p. 1.)

The ten years 1868-1878 were occupied chiefly with religious and literary subjects. In 1878 he returned to politics with the address at the London Institution on "Equality." From then until 1881 he wrote chiefly on Irish questions. From 1881 to 1886, his time was filled by a third visit to the Continent on education enquiries, and a visit to America. During this time politics were suspended, but as soon as he was free in 1886 he returned to Irish questions and continued writing thereon until his death in 1888. The noticeable facts are first that he showed a continuous interest in politics, for he left off writing only for the sake of more immediate professional work, and that the larger part of his political work was concerned with Ireland.

After 1878 almost the whole of his political work is on Ireland. Following the chronological order we shall have a natural arrangement of his writings. We must note that Arnold's apprenticeship to public life began with his appointment in 1847 as private secretary to Lord Lansdowne, a member of Lord John Russell's ministry. His letters at that time show signs of political interest. He attended a Chartist Convention in April 1848, and was induced to do some political writing at that time, but it was some years before Politics called him.

The first step was a pamphlet published in 1859, called " England and the Italian Question." Hitherto Arnold had published only poetry ; he still held the chair of Poetry at Oxford. He had travelled abroad considerably, in France and Switzerland in 1857, in Switzerland in 1858, and in France, Belgium, Switzerland and Piedmont in 1859, to report on elementary education. It was during this last visit in 1859, that he wrote and published the pamphlet—his first public prose— " England and the Italian Question."

The materials for this were collected during the enquiry into the systems of Popular Education on the Continent during 1859. The first mention of it occurs in a letter written at Strasbourg, wherein he says, " I shall put together for a pamphlet or for Fraser a sort of résumé of the present question as the result of what I have thought, read, and observed here about it." (Letter to Miss Arnold, 25th June 1859. Vol. I, p. 95.)

The events which immediately preceded were as follows. Arnold left England in March 1859. On 23rd April the demand of the Austrians that Sardinia should disarm was refused ; they

then crossed the Ticino.   During May and June
risings of the Italians took place at Florence,
Palma, Modena, Bologna.   The French arrived,
and on 4th June the Austrians were beaten at
Magenta, and at Solferino on 24th June.   The
Peace of Villafranca was signed on 11th July,
and the Treaty of Zurich in November.   Arnold's
pamphlet was published in the beginning of August,
that is to say, between the time when the astonishing
arrangement between Francis Joseph and Napoleon
was first made public by the Peace of Villafranca
and its ratification in the Treaty of Zurich.   Arnold
was in a good position to understand continental
feeling on the question.   At Paris he saw the
troops setting out for Lyons.   At Strasbourg we
find the first mention of the intended pamphlet.
It is really a plea for the independence of Italy
based upon the history of Italy.   Arnold praised
French action.   But in this, as in some of his letters
of this period, there are prophecies as to the future
which were certainly not verified, although his
statement that Alsace must always be French
has been justified recently by the treaty of Versailles.

Arnold's Report ·upon the systems of popular
education in France, Holland, and the French
Cantons of Switzerland in 1859 was issued as a
parliamentary paper in 1861.   It was reprinted
in the same year with an introduction.   This
Introduction itself was reprinted in " Mixed Essays"

in 1879, under the title "Democracy." This essay was Arnold's second piece of political writing. Sir Joshua Fitch says that "Arnold had been profoundly impressed by reading 'De Tocqueville.'" (Thomas and Matthew Arnold, p. 202.) In the style of this essay there is a curious and unusual formality quite different from the free, conversational tone characteristic of Arnold's prose, but at this distance of time the matter is still engaging. Most of Arnold's ideas, afterwards worked out and reiterated in one book after another, are to be found here—germs of thought later developed into his complete work on State action and on the composition of English Society. With one's eyes upon the Collectivist legislation of the last few years, we may say that this essay establishes Arnold's insight. It is a plea for more extended State action, especially in regard to Education. The line of argument is that by natural causes power has passed from the aristocracy to the middle class, that it is therefore necessary to give to English Democracy high reason and fine culture, always characteristics of the best democracies. To do this the middle class must encourage State action. To those who say that the State can be no better than the capacity of its individual citizens Arnold answers, first, that the State has access to wider sources of information, and that the habit of dealing with large affairs tends to produce enlargement of mind; and second, that Democracy has the choice of its own officials, and will be to blame if State action is unsatisfactory.

The prescience of this article is remarkable and has been overlooked by the critics of Arnold's politics. This was 1861, six years before the Reform Act of 1867. As for the plea on behalf of State action, the main feature of English political history of the last fifty years has been its accomplishment. Let us compare Arnold's ideal of politics and Professor Dicey's account of legislation in this century. Professor Dicey divides the legislation of the 19th century into three periods, the period of Blackstonian optimism (1800-1832), the period of Benthamite individualism (1820-1855), the period of Collectivism (1850-1900). Now this last period covers the time since the publication of Arnold's essay. Without saying that he had influence we certainly see that the legislation of the latter part of the century followed exactly the direction which Arnold desired. The ideal of the State representing and operating as the Best Self of the community appears five years after in the " Culture and Anarchy " Essays. We shall see later that Arnold's educational work on the political side is a continuous advocacy of State action towards the establishment of Secondary Education. Yet Professor Saintsbury says that Arnold " had no ideas, no first principles on politics at all." After the publication of the Report to which the essay on Democracy was the introduction, Arnold's published writings, up to 1866, were on literary subjects, although he still felt drawn by political interests. For example, to Mr. M. E. Grant-Duff, M.P. (since Sir M. E. Grant-Duff), on 24th May 1864, he wrote :

> " One is from time to time seized and irresistibly carried along by a temptation to treat political, or religious, or social matters, directly; but after yielding to such a temptation I always feel myself recoiling again, and disposed to touch them only so far as they can be touched through poetry."—(" Letters," Vol. I, p. 233.)

But in 1865 he was appointed on a second commission to enquire into the systems of education for the middle and upper classes in France, Italy, Germany and Switzerland. He returned from this commission in October 1865, and immediately went back to politics as he did in " Democracy," after the 1859 commission. During 1866-1868, " Friendship's Garland " and " Culture and Anarchy " were written. We have already considered these among his social writings, with the exception of the last chapter, that on " Our Liberal Practitioners." Some notice is given to it here because it is the point at which Arnold's social ideals came into direct contact with politics, and because here we see his attitude to contemporary political parties. He had been accused of not lending a helping hand

to the practical reformers, in other words, the
Liberal politicians of his time. But this he will
not do, he says, because upon examining their
proposed operations he finds that their projected
reforms are not what they appear to be, and comes
to the conclusion that it is better to go on en-
lightening his countrymen in his own way than
to help to carry these so called reforms. Of the
Liberal items he selects :

> Irish Church Disestablishment.
> The Real Estate Intestacy Bill.
> Marriage with a Deceased Wife's Sister.
> Free Trade.

The first and third of these are completed, and,
so far as Liberalism is concerned, unassailable.
By their fruits they are judged. And by this same
judgment which so entirely approves them Arnold
himself is judged. For although he did not attack
the actual reforms, yet he did attack the motives
behind them. Hence we feel the absence of the
frank attack or the frank defence, and a half hidden
consciousness of justice and victory on the Liberal
side. Arnold's antipathy to the Liberal doctrine
of Free Trade arose from the fact that he
thought the cheapness of food produced a
too great increase of population, and hence
social misery. He did not attack it from
the economic side in the direction, for instance,

taken since Mr. Joseph Chamberlain's advocacy of Tariff Reform. Yet Arnold's criticism certainly touched a black spot attributable to our system of Free Trade. The Real Estates Intestacy Bill proposed that when a man died without leaving a will his land should not go entirely to the eldest son but should be divided equally amongst all the children ; the object being to strike at the exclusive possession of the land by the aristocracy. Again we see Arnold's inconsistent attitude ; for at a later time he criticised the inequalities in our society caused by the existing system of inheriting property.

Since the plea for equality is one of the prominent positive elements in Arnold's politics, one would have thought that this Bill would commend itself to Arnold. But not so. He found fault with the reasoning upon which it was founded—the notion that children have natural rights to the equal enjoyment of their father's property—and thus attacks what certainly was a movement in the direction of equality. " Politics is one long second best," said John Morley : and a practical politician holding Arnold's views would have accepted as much as the Real Estates Intestacy Bill offered and would have worked and waited for more, instead of taking a position dialectically defensible but impossible to a practical reformer working in Politics.

Arnold's position in the matter is indeed curiously inconsistent with what followed, for after this he wrote nothing on Politics for ten years. A second series of political writings began with an address at the Royal Institution in 1878 on Equality, wherein he advocated in his most persuasive manner this very principle of Equality. Prof. Saintsbury names this essay as an example of the un-English side of Arnold (" Matthew Arnold," p. 172). It is, and it is a fair instance also of applying new ideas to stock habits—and of a certain reforming strain in him—the positive side of his critical spirit. This address is based upon a maxim of Menander : " Choose equality and flee greed." It is a plea for social equality, and rests its case on the general praise passed by observers on the French nation, especially the French peasantry. Arnold first cites the deeply rooted disbelief of the English in equality. He then compares the law on the Continent relating to bequest, by which a tendency to equality is produced ; the law in the colonies and in America; and shows that in France and in the French provinces of Germany, Belgium and Italy, and in the three most important Cantons of Switzerland entirely, and mainly in all the others, the Code Napoleon is the law; the law which " leaves a man free to dispose of but one-fourth of his property, of whatever kind, if he have three children or more, of one-third if he have two children, or a half if he have but one child." In America the practice is against entail; in Australia a regulation prevents a proprietor holding a landed estate of more than a certain value. Arnold, however, fixes on France. Here he says, you have a fine standard of social manners, one of the advances in humanisation : but this fine standard of social manners is not possible where great inequalities of social conditions are present.

It is just here that we see the central aim of Arnold's efforts in politics, the establishment of a social system of agreeableness and refinement, the labourer entering into conversation quite easily, " sustaining his part in a perfectly becoming way, with a pleasant combination of dignity and quiet humour ; " a social system full of the goodness and agreeableness of life, humanisation, civilisation. This it is which characterises Arnold as a social reformer, that while other men have insisted upon economic reform and the fairer distribution of wealth, or political reform and a larger share of power for the artisan class, he had his eye fixed upon a social ideal. What Liberals and the Socialists will say is that this ideal social system can only come by the path of political or economic change. Arnold praised French society, yet France was not, when Arnold was writing, a favourable witness for the results of equality. Arnold's reply is that French " deterioration and intellectual stoppage " are due to " a failing and feeble hold upon the power of conduct," and not the result of their social equality. He then repeats the criticism of " Culture and Anarchy " upon our three classes, and sums up our love of inequality by saying that it is " the vulgarity in us and the brutality admiring and worshipping the splendid materiality." The question arises, how did Arnold propose to alter this inequality? Certainly he adopts the proposal of John Stuart Mill to pass a " law of bequest fixing the maximum whether of land or money, which any one individual may take by bequest or inheritance." It is true that in this address he still described the Real Estates Intestacy Bill as puerile, yet in advocating J. S. Mill's reform of the law of bequest there was surely no great difference.

Politics, at any rate, which, as John Morley said, is one's second best, will not admit such fine distinctions, and no reform has come otherwise than by accepting one half, if the whole is impossible. We may not leave the essay without reference to the new illustrations which he introduces of the middle and Puritan class. For whatever we think of the argument from particulars the reading on pages 79-84, with reference to beauty and manner and Puritanism, is in Arnold's most engaging manner. His plan in this essay really amounts to a more equitable distribution of wealth ; it is made, doubtless, with an ideal of social development

before him, through economic changes. That
it is which links him to later developments of
Liberalism and by this advocacy of State action
links him with Socialism. These connections,
shall we say, with the future, are curious in a nature
so aristocratic, and for a temperament usually
and wrongly regarded as dilettante. " Irish
Catholicism and British Liberalism " is independent,
novel and positive. It is a plea for what is now an
accomplished fact—a Catholic university in Ireland,
and deals with this subject in a comprehensive
way. Arnold's argument is that Catholic France
allowed the Protestants of Alsace to have the
Protestant University of Strasbourg ; and
Protestant Prussia allows the Catholics of the Rhine
Province to have the Catholic University of Bonn.
J. S. Mill, and John Morley at that time, are in
favour of it : Mr. Chamberlain and Sir Charles
Dilke voted for it. Yet the mass of the Liberals are
against it, because they represent the middle class,
and the middle class, which is Puritan, will have
nothing to do with Popery. Justice, however, should
be done. Secondary education also should be given
to Ireland and a University with Catholic professors
appointed by Government officials. Arnold then
passes eulogy upon the Roman Catholic Church
for its history and its embodiment of a great past,
and for its beauty and poetry. He expresses
firmly his approbation of the votes of Mr. Chamber-

lain and Sir Charles Dilke—that is of what was then the most advanced section of the Liberal party. On this matter Arnold followed Burke, who advocated the extension of educational opportunities to the Roman Catholic clergy and resisted the argument that the Protestant universities were open to Roman Catholics. " The theological opinions and peculiar right of one religion never can be properly taught in universities founded for the purposes and on the principles of another, which in many points are directly opposite."— (" Edmund Burke on Irish Affairs," p. 194.)

There is an interesting statement in this article of Arnold's position towards the Liberal party. " I prefer to remember only that their cause is, in a general way, at any rate, mine also ; that I serve and would fain follow the Liberal ideal."

In February 1879, appeared the address given to the Ipswich Working Men's College, entitled " Ecce Convertimur ad Gentes." Therein were advocated the three articles named above. This is a noticeable address because in it there is the nearest possible approach to the tone of the demagogue. There is something of the tone of the Collectivist, some foreshadowing of the Socialist inrush. " We turn to the Gentiles," he exclaims. After twenty years vainly endeavouring to teach the middle class he appeals to the working class. To take up the work and carry it forward was hardly in Arnold's line. It shows a temporary loss of faith in the process of sowing the seed, which, he said, was his part in the work of progress, temporary let us say, because this appeal was not repeated.

The general election of 1880 then took place and the Liberals came in triumphant. Mr. Knowles, the editor of the *Nineteenth Century*, appears to have asked Arnold for an article which appeared in the July number, entitled " The Future of Liberalism." In this article attack is made once more upon civilisation in England, and especially upon the Liberals because while satisfying the instinct for expansion, for example, by free trade and liberty, they have not satisfied the instinct for manners and for knowledge for the middle class. The Tories have this and the Liberals have that, but neither party works for humanisation. He again attacks the Liberals for their advocacy of the Burials Bill, the Deceased Wife's Sister Bill, and for the first time Local Option, urging that the advance of civilisation will not be made in a true way by these measures. The new note of this criticism, however, —and it is welcome here because although it did appear in Arnold's criticism of English life, yet it never appeared enough—is the condemnation of the over-crowded manufacturing centres such as Bolton and Wigan, and the distress ensuing upon the over-production caused by unscrupulous capitalists

hasting to be rich. Arnold was writing in the flood
tide of Liberal success, but he foretells that the
Liberal measures will be found wanting, that the
Tories will return to power : and only when the
Liberals understand and practise the true and
noble sciences of Ethics and Politics will they
become permanently established in power. Important in this article is the indication of Arnold's
interest in Irish politics. From this date, excepting
his last article on Welsh Disestablishment, all
his political work was on Ireland. The writings
are divided naturally into two portions :

1. Those which were written in 1881 after
   Mr. Gladstone's victory of 1880, when the
   Parnell dominance arose, and a Land Bill
   and a Coercion Bill were in the air.
2. Those which were written in 1886 and 1887,
   after Mr. Gladstone's Home-Rule proposals.

In April and June 1881, appeared two articles
entitled " The Incompatibles." At the same time
he edited Burke's " Letters, Speeches and Tracts
on Irish Affairs." To Burke he ascribed the
positive side of his Irish policy. The phrase
" Our measures must be healing " which sounded
again and again in the " Irish Essays " and formed
the text of Arnold's advice to English politicians, is
Burke's. But from the point in time at which we

now stand Burke's Irish work has only a historical and literary interest. All of the questions with which he deals are quieted and the language ranges around what are now but names and episodes. The iniquity of the Popery laws, the Catholic disabilities, the need for concurrent endowment, the restrictions on trade, the Government's resistance to fair claims, its surrender to insurrection, the identity of Irish interests with English interests—these form the subjects of Burke's " Speeches and Letters."

What is fine in Burke on the one side is his attachment to great and sound principles, his temper and discrimination; and, on the other side, his insistence upon positive reforms dealing with flagrant inequalities and injustice, his firm sense of order and law, and that is exactly Arnold's point of view. Irritating to the party politician, paradoxical to the man in the street, in wisdom and in justice Arnold is above them both. In the articles of 1881, " The Incompatibles," Arnold was suggestive and constructive. He saw clearly Irish grievances and made an attempt to remedy them on his own lines. He admits them fully : the material grievance that the tenant lost the benefit of the improvements which he had made, the moral grievance that the landlord system was one of conquest, confiscation, ill-usage, misgovernment, and tyranny. The first part of " The Incompa-

o

tibles " was written in April 1881, before the provisions of the Land Act of that year were known, the second part in June, after they had been announced. But he saw that the system which it established could not be permanent. Such as the Bill was, Arnold accepted it. The curious thing is the proposal that England should break with the past by a "striking and solemn act—the expropriation of bad landlords." A commission was to sit and draw up three lists of bad landlords—

> "And taking twenty-five years' purchase as the ordinary selling price of an Irish estate, to expropriate the least bad of the three classes of scheduled landlords at twenty years' purchase, the next class at fifteen years' purchase, the worst at ten years' purchase."

For the commission he suggested Lord Coleridge and Mr. Samuel Morley. A second commission was to be formed to deal with the question of religion, "to make amends for our abominable treatment of it under the long reign of the penal code." Lord Coleridge was selected for this and the other Mr. Morley, Mr. John Morley. This was Arnold's proposal for dealing directly and immediately with the Land Question. But he traced the Irish Question, as he traced the Condition of England question, to our bad civilisation and specially to our bad middle class civilisation; hence

he sees that the real healing treatment of Ireland
must come by the reform of our own civilisation
and the showing of the best side of our nation
to the Irish. The aim was in Arnold's mind to
secure peace with Ireland, by making our national
character attractive to Ireland. We must re-fashion
it so that a blending of the two nations may be made
possible : as Wales and Scotland have become
almost perfectly blended with England. This was
not exactly politics ; nor was the suggestion that
the Irish should be made acquainted with the
politer elements in English society quite serious
enough a remedy for Ireland's ills.

Five years after the publication of " Irish Essays "
Arnold turned to Ireland again. In the interval he
visited America and delivered his American Lectures
—published as " Numbers." It is well to observe
this, as it provides one of the chief keys to Arnold's
opinions, and co-ordinates much and probably most
of his political ideas, and allies him most to existing
events in British politics. In this respect he started
and supported and pushed on views of State action
which gave a rational basis to the characteristic
feature of later 19th century legislation. Arnold
was really a Collectivist.

We may here notice also two articles on America,
one contributed before he had visited America.
" A Word about America," the *Nineteenth Century*,
May, 1882, and one after his first visit, " A Word

more about America," the *Nineteenth Century*, February 1885. They are both written in the style of " Culture and Anarchy " and apply the class description of English Society to America. The principal contention of the first is that America is England without the lower and without the upper class. The second article adds other things, but the feature of interest is the almost prophetic vision of modern Imperialism and constitutional reform. These, however, are the sidepaths of Arnold's work. He visited America a second time in 1886. Soon after, two articles followed in *Murray's Magazine*, January and February 1887, on General Grant. His nephew, Edward Arnold, was then Editor of *Murray's*, and this explains the appearance of these articles which have but slight interest. He ranges over a wide ground of Drama and Literature, wrote some poetry, and then in 1886, joined in the political excitement aroused by the Home Rule question. Arnold followed these political movements in five articles published between May 1886, and March 1888. These articles have the melancholy interest of being among the last of Arnold's work. They show him to us in the field of party politics. The fine distinctions of the literary world are lost. The highly tempered weapons of ironic insight and persiflage avail little here. Moderation, appreciation of the opposite side, understanding the rationale of an adversary—these are misunderstood in this world.

These articles are melancholy and characteristic, but not the most interesting of his work. Politics did not give to Arnold scope for the exercise of his master gift. The prose is clear, and the familiar versatility and élan and raciness are there, but there is not that calm and sure mastery of his subject— that judgment—which in the " Essays on Criticism " carries us unresisting with him. There the finest critical insight shines steadily through every line. Here in the " Nadir of Liberalism " and the "Zenith of Conservatism " he is merely a gentleman expressing his political views and, we will say, his political bias. His Home Rule articles, as we may call them, are typical of his mind, but could satisfy no party man. The blinded attitude of the partisan was not his. Illuminating it always will be to see politics as a fine spirit sees them ; and to get them in a finer literary expression than that of the average politician.

But a statesman is a statesman, and Doctor Harvey's remark upon Bacon's criticism of him : " He wrote upon science like a Lord Chancellor," has a wide application. Arnold in literature was superb and supreme. These political articles are simply notes. We saw that in 1868, while calling himself a Liberal, he attacked such a great Liberal measure as the Irish Church Disestablishment

Bill and also the working of Free Trade. In 1886 he retains the name of Liberal—a Liberal of the future—but he has gone over entirely to the Conservative side, with special favour for the Liberal Unionists. His polite cuffs are for the Liberals and the Liberal leaders ; his praises—not exuberant— for the Conservatives and the Conservative leaders. This is a fragment on Mr. Gladstone :

> "The reason why Mr. Gladstone has not succeeded hitherto in the real and high work of a statesman is that he is in truth not a statesman, properly so called, at all, but an unrivalled parliamentary leader and manager."—(" Nadir of Liberalism," *Nineteenth Century*, May, 1886.)

The democracy is featherbrained and Lord Hartington seems to be the ideal statesman.

" The Nadir of Liberalism " was published in the *Nineteenth Century*, May 1886. It was written during the short life of the parliament which assembled on January 12th, 1886, Mr. Gladstone being Prime Minister, and was dissolved on June 26th, 1886. " The Nadir of Liberalism " is a criticism of the Liberal foreign policy which, Arnold said, had everywhere on the Continent lowered the prestige of England. He makes a comparison of the success which attended Bismarck's policy with the failure which attended Mr. Gladstone's. Mr. Gladstone, as we have already seen, he designated as a parliamentary genius,

a politician but not a statesman. The full recognition of Mr. Gladstone's gifts is followed by
such strokes as this : " He does not foresee
danger. Statesmen foresee, Mr. Gladstone does
not." (p. 657.) Arnold contested the Home
Rule Bill with the familiar arguments that it would
loosen the political ties between England and
Ireland, and would hand over Ulster to the Catholics.
He proposed, as an alternative plan, to give Ireland
three local legislatures, following the lines of its
three natural divisions :

> Ulster or British Ireland.
> Leinster or Metropolitan Ireland.
> Munster and Connaught or Celtic Ireland.

Irish members were still to sit in the Imperial
Parliament.

On the question of Catholicism Arnold would
have allowed each of these legislatures to establish
its own religion. Mr. Gladstone's Disestablishment Bill did not allow the Irish power to establish
their own preference in religion. On the land
question he frankly says that the Irish landlord
system cannot be maintained, and that in the loss involved in purchasing them out, England should
share. This of course is now accomplished. After
the dissolution of the twelfth parliament, 1886,
a general election took place in July, by which Lord
Salisbury was returned to power, taking office

on August 3rd.   The second session of this parliament met on 27th January 1887.   It was almost entirely occupied by Irish affairs and was one of the longest and stormiest and most indecorous for many years.   The "Zenith of Conservatism" (*Nineteenth Century*, January 1887) is really an exhortation to the Liberal Unionists and Conservatives to stand firm, and work out a policy of which he gives four points :

1.   Procedure in the House of Commons.   The power of closure which he advocated here was established soon after.

2.   Local Government.   This was as we have seen in " Ecce Convertimur ad Gentes," continuously advocated by Arnold.   He thought that Liberals and Conservatives might co-operate.   In May 1886, he pointed out that it was in neither the Liberal nor the Conservative programmes. Again in January 1887, he recommends it to the Conservatives ; and draws good examples of it from Russia and America.   Since Arnold's time this reform has been accomplished by the Parish Councils Bills.

3.   Church Disestablishment in Wales.   Arnold saw plainly the absurdity of a Church Establishment for the small minority in Wales, and wished the Conservatives to

undertake a constructive reform. The Liberals would only destroy ; for vital reform they had " little disposition and no faculty." To this question he devoted an entire article, the last political essay he wrote, March 1888, National Disestablishment in Wales.

4. Ireland. This is the main subject of the four articles ; they deal with the administration of the law, the government and the land system.

A. ADMINISTRATION OF THE LAW.

The emphasis of the appeal to the Conservative is upon establishment of order and respect for the law, by administrative firmness if possible, if not by a Coercion Act. He condemned the Government's action in regard to evictions which had been carried out weakly and vacillatingly. He desired the suppression of the inflammatory speeches by the Irish leaders.

B. GOVERNMENT.

In January in " The Nadir of Liberalism " Arnold had declared against the Home Rule proposals. He reintroduces as a parallel to Home Rule the separate congresses of the Northern and Southern States.

C. The Land System.

He attacks in particular Lord Clanricarde with
his 50,000 acres. " Lord Clanricarde, 'mere land-
merchant,' living, we are told, in the Albany,
contemptuous and neglectful, never going near his
tenants, never hearing what they have to ask or
say, doing nothing at all for them, is an absurdity,
and therefore cannot now long be maintained." We
have seen already in the " Irish Essays " his proposals for the expropriation of bad landlords.
He attacks the Land Act of 1881, in that it confirmed
the divided ownership and never recognised the
distinction between good landlord and bad. The
articles " Up to Easter," " From Easter to August,"
follow the lines here taken. On 21st February
1887, Mr. W. H. Smith introduced new rules of
procedure, as the first business of the new government ; these became on 18th March a standing
order of the House. On 1st April the Criminal
Law (Ireland) Amendment Bill was read a first
time and passed on 8th July. The Crimes Act
was introduced, and an Act dealing with the
omissions of the Land Act of 1881, entitled an
Act to amend the Land Law (Ireland) Act, 1881,
and the Purchase of Land (Ireland) Act, 1885.
Local government for England was not dealt with
then, nor the Church Establishment in Wales, nor
was any new system of Irish Government established.

" Up to Easter," *Nineteenth Century*, May 1887, is a defence of the Coercion Act, although Arnold would have preferred administrative action rather than special legislation. He brings in quotations from the Irish leaders to show the revolutionary temper of the agitation, but at the same time he advises measures for meeting the Irish grievances. A parallel to this he finds in Provence, which is a separate nationality but united with France. He suggests that local government is needed both for Great Britain and Ireland. He proposes also that there should be for Ireland two legislatures : one for the Protestant North and one for the Catholic South : and on the land question, the establishment of single ownership.

" From Easter to August " *Nineteenth Century*, September 1887. There is discontent with the Conservatives for not passing remedial measures and for wavering in their administration of Ireland. The " great force of quiet, reasonable opinion throughout the country " is beginning to be dissatisfied with the Conservative performances.

Arnold calls again for a firm administration of the law, and if necessary, the suppression of the Land League. He attacks the government Land Bill, which was introduced into the House of Lords on March 31st, but was not passed until July 4th. It passed the Commons Committee in an altered form on August 3rd, and became law only at the end of the session in September. Of it Arnold says, " The measure was neither frank, firm, simple, nor healing." He then turns upon the landlords, of whom he finds three types : " the insolent landlord, the exacting landlord, the beggared landlord." Arnold's point is that the Government has lost ground by their action in the evictions, and by the weakness of the Land Bill, and he seemed to anticipate the near time when " the quiet reasonable people, the Liberals of the Nadir, will be swept away, and the new democracy will pass over their body." That anticipation was soon to be fulfilled. There is to this article one of those beautiful conclusions of which Arnold gave so many examples, and none better than this.

The political writings were finished, indeed nearly all his writing was finished when the *National Review* article on Disestablishment in Wales appeared in March, 1888. Happy phrases, old and new are here ; the looking to the Continent for examples, the old argument, the insistence on the need to deal with actual grievances, not in the negative way, the way of the Liberals, but to deal with them. The grievance in Wales, he admits, is that the Established Church there is not in accord with the religion of the majority of the community there. He advises the Conservatives, therefore, not to attempt to uphold the Establishment in Wales just as it is, but suggests the plan of France and Germany, where the churches are established according to the preferences of the people.

An account is given of the settlement in Germany by the Treaty of Westphalia in 1648, by which the Church and property in the possession of the Catholic or the Lutheran or the Zwinglian parties on the 1st January 1624, should remain with them. Arnold proposed that this plan should be adopted in Wales : where the people are of the Presbyterian faith, let the churches and tithe pass to them ; where the Anglican Church has taken hold, let the churches with all the cathedrals remain to the Anglicans. In Presbyterian districts Presbyterian ministers should be appointed and everywhere the parish should have the power of veto. The division of the districts was to be left in the hands of a commission, for which Arnold suggested two Lords, a Bishop, and Mr. Henry Richard. Very little difficulty would be here, Arnold thought, if once the equity of the case were brought home to people's minds. " It is a matter to be referred to fair and intelligent men, of whom, happily, we have plenty, whom one could quite trust to carry honestly into effect a distribution of which the principle was understood and accepted by them." This is great faith in human reasonableness. But let us repeat that this is the question in politics which aroused deep feeling, and dealt with the most sensitive of vested interests, religion and property.

A commission may sit to make enquiries upon some public matter, or even to settle the boundaries of new municipalities, but surely no politician would propose that such a transfer as Arnold proposed, of churches and church property, should be made— much less made in this way. Yet he saw clearly the grievance, which in a few years was settled by the actual Disestablishment of the Church.

Much of Arnold's political writing dealt with controversies now dead. Some things he fought against have come to pass. The Irish question appears to be solved. Many party discontents have been obliterated, and since the Great War the questions raised by Arnold appear to have receded further. But there remains one thing, to bring into emphasis Arnold's doctrine of the State : the State as the organ of the community, of the best self of the community. We have seen this doctrine applied to Education. We have seen it in his criticism of society. And although his political writings are nearly all on particular topics treating less of general principles, yet the sense of the State, of the nation as a whole, is clearly felt. On every question it is the decisive factor in his judgment, a pervading principle, and fashions all his conclusions. Hence, for instance, his plea for a Roman Catholic University for Ireland, and his opposition to Disestablishment in Wales. The individual, the section, the group, has to give way before the paramount claim of the larger whole.

Arnold derived this principle from his father, and specially refers to it in a letter to his mother, "Letters, Vol. I, p. 226 : " In my notions about the State I am quite papa's son, and his continuator. I often think of this—the more so because in this direction he has had so few who felt with him. But I inherit from him a deep sense of what, in the Greek and Roman world, was sound and rational." And again to her, p. 381, Vol. I, " Letters."

In view of the fact that this doctrine of the State was so marked a principle of all Arnold's work, it is important to see how one generation laid its hand on another.

RELIGION

BIBLIOGRAPHY

1863. Dean Stanley's Lectures on the Jewish Church.
1869. "St. Paul and Protestantism."
1870. "Puritanism and the Church of England."
      "St. Paul and Protestantism," in volume.
1871. "Literature and Dogma," *Cornhill Magazine*, July and October.
1872. "A Bible Reading for Schools." (Isaiah, chapters 40-66.)
1873. "Literature and Dogma."
1874. Review of objections to "Literature and Dogma." Various articles afterwards published in "God and the Bible."
1875. "God and the Bible."
      The Great Prophecy of Israel's Restoration.
1877. "Last Essays."
1883. "Isaiah of Jerusalem."
1887. "A Friend of God."

ARNOLD was born in his father's School-house at Laleham and lived there until his sixth year, 1828, when Dr. Arnold went to Rugby. Here he lived until he was sixteen, and then went to Winchester. Dean Stanley has given us glimpses

of the family life of the Arnolds, and it is these
influences which shaped Matthew Arnold's character. The whole family was marked by a deep
seriousness. Above all, Mrs. Arnold's saintly
life shines clear, and her children have honoured
her memory. We know Matthew Arnold's mind
fully. In addition to his letters we have his note-
books, and these are a surprising witness to the
deeply religious disposition of his mind. Having
abandoned supernatural Christianity, having abandoned Christianity altogether, as some would say,
yet to the close of his life he observed the forms
of worship. These things must be remembered
in order to see and measure the kind and extent
of Arnold's influence on religious life and thought.
He had in reality a deeply spiritual mind.

His first work, poetry published before
he was thirty, is full, poignantly full, of signs of a
change from belief in supernatural Christianity
to that naturalistic religion which later he advocated.
His poetry indicates the rejection of early beliefs,
and when the first of his published letters was
written the change is completed. There in the
poetry are the deep marks of an intellectual anguish,
of a breaking of bonds of love and reverence for
old things riven by the inexorable conquerors,
light, reason, irony : no invective, nothing but
the keen pain of relinquishing a precious possession ;
so precious that he holds on to the gift through all

intellectual change, so precious that to the very end he adheres to the forms and the language of the very creed which he has abandoned. We may regret that no diaries show us the steps by which Arnold made the passage out of orthodoxy. Yet nothing in Arnold's intellectual history had such shaping power on his work as this change. It permeates his poetry and fills his most pathetic utterances. It stimulated him to write three or four of his most powerful books. It drew on him suspicion, aversion, censure. It drew on him, too, the intellectual affection of every man who has made the same passage. And behind the Arnold who has rejected the old Christian conceptions is the pathetic figure passing through doubt. In " Literature and Dogma " he is serene and certain enough, but the poetry reminds us of his past. Herein was the attraction of Arnold for his generation. Such smiling certainty he shows, yet we cannot forget the unspoken labour.

Arnold very soon showed interest in religious questions. His mind was moving in many directions, and there were outside influences stimulating his religious interests. In 1859 he met Renan. In 1860, " Essays and Reviews " was published. In 1866 " Ecce Homo," and in January 1863, then forty-one, Arnold published an article in *Macmillan's Magazine*, " The Bishop and the Philosopher," dealing with a recently issued transla-

tion of Spinoza's "Tractatus Theologico-Politicus."
In the February number of the same magazine he
published a review of Dean Stanley's "Lectures
on the Jewish Church." In December came
"A Word more about Spinoza"—parts of the two
articles being published later in Essays in Criticism.
These two articles on Spinoza mark the entrance of
Arnold into the realm of religious thought, and they
have this interest for us, that we see at once most of
Arnold's main ideas. We may note here that
recent editors of Spinoza have attributed to Arnold's
articles a certain revival of interest in Spinoza and,
what is of great importance, we see in these articles
a clue to one of the principal constructive influences
of Arnold's mind. We shall refer later to the
correspondence with Cardinal Newman in which
Arnold gives the names of the four men to whom he
owed most. Among them was Goethe, and in these
Spinoza articles we can see what he drew from
Goethe, and how this was related to his Words-
worthian mind. Arnold did not at any time
devote himself directly to Goethe by way of exposition, although references are frequent enough.
But in this Spinoza article he states Goethe's
doctrine of Nature. At this point therefore we
see the way in which Arnold received the Goethe
influence, and its connection with Wordsworth.
The subject has recently been treated in detail
and with most careful criticism by Mr. J. B. Orrick

("Matthew Arnold and Goethe," J. B. Orrick, English Goethe Society).

The main idea of these two articles is that the mere insistence upon negative, critical, destructive conclusions is not enough. He raises the question : Does it edify ? Hence the appreciation of Colenso's work ; and hence frequently depreciation of his own very allies. This is one of the peculiar characteristics of Arnold; it is one of the recurring notes of his writing, and the very thing which in the eyes of many gives a note of insincerity. He accepts Bishop Coleman's conclusions, and goes on :

"What then ? What follows from all this ? What change is it, if true, to produce in the relations of mankind to the Christian religion ? If the old theory of Scripture inspiration is to be abandoned, what place is the Bible henceforth to hold among books ? What is the new Christianity to be like ? How are governments to deal with National Churches founded to maintain a very different conception of Christianity ? "

In comparison with Colenso, Arnold selected Spinoza. The first English translation of the "Tractatus Theologico-Politicus" was published at this time, and was the occasion of Arnold's articles. Neither the interest in Colenso nor in Spinoza is great, and the value of this first essay of Arnold consists in the curious but characteristic depreciation of purely critical work. This is the note to be heard again and again. We turn back

to the article, " Dean Stanley's Lectures on the
Jewish Church," which comes in between the
Spinoza articles. Very little notice has been given
by Arnold's biographers to this essay; yet it should
receive attention. There is a note of passion in
it rarely heard. It shows the deep feeling underlying Arnold's view of religion ; it shows how
ardently he wished to build a way from supernatural to natural Christianity ; it shows the profoundly religious element in his nature, and it
seems like a loud and solemn call to a new and real
and rational interpretation of Christianity. A
space of six years follows before Arnold began
his well-known essays on religion, before " St.
Paul and Protestantism." In that six years appeared the literary essays in " Essays in Criticism "
and then " Culture and Anarchy." His mind
was now mature and producing continuously
great work. He felt that he was becoming
more and more known, and that his public influence
was increasing. Thus from social subjects he
enters the theological world. He came to it by a
natural transition when considering the working
principles of society.

If the reader will look into " Culture and Anarchy"
he will find Arnold analysing society into three
classes, Barbarians, Philistines, Populace, and then
by the working principles, Hebraism and Hellenism.
In doing this we find him occupied with St. Paul's

interpretation of Christianity ; and then with the Puritan mishandling of his ideas. " Culture and Anarchy " is a plea for Hellenism and a criticism of Hebraism. " St. Paul and Protestantism" is a plea for true Hebraism. In fact " St. Paul and Protestantism," " Culture and Anarchy," " Literature and Dogma," are united by one continuous idea. Among his first writings on religious subjects was an essay in the *Cornhill Magazine*, February 1870, " Puritanism in the Church of England," afterwards published in " St. Paul and Protestantism." A letter of 13th November 1869, shows the ideas in his mind. His father had helped to introduce new views of inspiration ; and he himself hoped to change the notions of justification. This was specially directed to what Arnold called the Puritan class: hence " St. Paul and Protestantism " is Arnold's rendering of St. Paul's theology with a view to correcting the mistakes of Nonconformity.

There was a positive side to Arnold and his letter shows it. " St. Paul and Protestantism " is thus the first expression of Arnold's religious ideas. It attacks the renderings of St. Paul's theology known as Calvinism and Arminianism. He fixes on the Westminster Confession and that of the Congregational Year Book as expressing Calvinistic Puritanism ; and on John Wesley and the *Methodist Magazine* as expressing Arminian Puritanism. The great doctrine of the former is

Predestination, and of the latter Justification.
Arnold points out that they both appeal to the Bible,
and especially to St. Paul.   He examines in detail
the doctrines of Faith, Original Sin, Predestination
and Justification. He sets off against these terms the
representation of St. Paul's ideas as being soundly
based upon his own personal experience, keeping
always in close contact with life, retaining but
few elements of supernaturalism and these only
in a secondary place, and drawing out with profound
truth the figure of Christ as the human Exemplar.

This criticism of Puritanism as to its misinter-
pretation of St. Paul was followed by the essay on
" Puritanism and the Church of England."   Of this
Arnold wrote, " The Bishop of Manchester, Dr.
Fraser, told me it had been startlingly new to him ;
but the more he thought of it, the more he thought
it was true." (" Letters " Vol. II, p. 38.)   In
this essay Arnold asserts that " only a few who have
searched out the matter know how far Nonconformity is due also to the Church of England's
invincible reluctance to narrow her large and loose
formularies to the strict Calvinistic sense dear to
Puritanism." The evidence in support of this
statement is given in the first part of the essay.
The chief data are :

1. The Lambeth Articles of 1595, which teach
   Calvinism, were recalled and suppressed.

2. The Catechism usually printed in English Bibles from 1552 containing statements of Calvinistic doctrine was removed in 1615.

3. At the Hampton Court Conference 1604, the Puritan foreman moved for the insertion of the Calvinistic Lambeth Articles in the Book of Articles. The Bishops refused.

4. It was a subject of complaint by the Puritans to the Committee of Divines appointed by the House of Lords, 1641, that Arminianism was being taught in the Church.

5. At the Savoy Conference, 1661, the Puritans complain again that the Liturgy is defective, that is, that it did not contain Calvinistic doctrine.

The foregoing is the evidence upon which Arnold founds his assertion that the Puritans endeavoured to fix the Church in Calvinistic doctrine, and that this tendency was resisted successfully by the natural desire within the Church for scope and development. Puritanism now no longer holds firmly Calvinistic doctrines. This emancipation, said Arnold, is due to the influence of the Church, quoting Henry More, Jeremy Taylor and Bishop Wilson. Nonconformists separated from the Church for opinions, and therefore they are fixed down more firmly to these opinions ; while the Church, not existing for the sake of opinions, has

larger scope for expansion. Arnold, using the
words of Cardinal Newman, then explains how
inevitably the principle of development must be at
work in the Church. The human mind was
incapable of comprehending the full meaning of
the revelation of the Gospel in Christ. Time was
required for its purport and significance to be
understood, time for this reason, that the fuller
interpretation of Divine truth is dependent upon
outer influences ; as, for example, the condition
of philosophy and science. Such periods as the early
and mediæval were unable to express adequately the
Gospel because to do this requires expression in the
terms of philosophy and science, and the state of
philosophy and science in those times was not such as
to provide permanent conceptions and statements
of Divine truth. Further, the purpose of the
Church is towards conduct, it is a corporation for
moral growth, and its members adopt those helps
which enable it to pursue these ends. In this way
and for this reason were developed discipline,
ritual, architecture, State connections, dogma.

The only justification for separation is when it
takes place on the ground of practice and not for
the sake of speculative opinions. The political
break up of the world at the time of the Reformation
was perhaps the reason for the setting up of a
distinctly National Church. Yet the Anglican
Church in separating from Rome declared that it

did so on the ground of immoral practice in the
Romish Church. Nonconformists, however, say
that the Anglican Church order is unscriptural :
that its doctrines of priestly absolution and the
Real Presence are unscriptural : that they themselves are determined to preach only the simple
Gospel. To this Arnold replies that the Anglican
Church does not claim that its Church order
is scriptural ; it has grown as needed; nor
does she insist on the doctrines of priestly
absolution and of the Real Presence. She
leaves room for development. On the other
hand, it may be said that just as much is the
doctrine of Justification a development from
Scripture. On these grounds, therefore, he
calls upon Nonconformists to unite with the Church
for real righteousness, for " Then might there arise a
mighty and undistracted power of joint life."
He gives in conclusion in seven articles Tillotson's
proposals for comprehension.

The Essay on " Modern Dissent " is particularly
acrid : acrid in Arnold's way. He states that the
characteristic doctrines of Puritanism are gradually
passing away. In their place, to justify its existence,
Dissent is urging the unscripturalness of Episcopacy.
Arnold then criticises Dissenters for lacking the
inward qualities of love, joy, peace, to secure
which, he says, Paul left the Puritans of his day.
A phrase occurring in a speech of Mr. Winter-

botham's, provides Arnold with a text for his attack upon Dissenters : " A spirit of watchful jealousy." He deals with the objections which Dissenters make to the proposal that they should re-enter the Church. Then follows a picture of Dissenting life which he describes as a feeding of the ordinary self through the machinery of their denominations in contrast to the Christian ideal of the annulment of self.

These three Essays, "St. Paul and Protestantism," " Puritanism and the Church of England," and " Modern Dissent," contain Arnold's criticism of the theology, the *raison d'être* and the character of Nonconformity. All his traditions were attached to the Church. Rationalist agnostic as he was, it was his intellectual convictions alone which separated him from the Church. His family, Oxford, his friends, his innate tendency to centrality, fixed his sympathies in the National Church. We shall see later that his intellectual views place a great distance between the orthodox Churchmen and himself : and yet he spoke as a member of the Church. He saw its worthy features : he entered into its great traditions : he shared in its legacies of training. So he spoke as a son, not as an outsider, as standing on neutral ground between Dissent and the Church. Doubtless he wished to do so : but in point of fact he never could speak otherwise than as inside the Church. It was impossible for him to approach the matter from an impartial point of view. Now we ask the question, was he right ?

We come first to the cause for which Non-conformists left the Church. Arnold says that they separated for the sake of one or more of the three doctrines, Predestination, Original Sin, Justification; that they separated for opinions. He goes further and asserts that the only justifiable ground for separation is a point of morals. The Puritan Churches, he says, separated for the sake of these three tenets. It is impossible to sustain this. Perfectly accurate it is to say that the Puritans held these doctrines firmly and advocated them persistently ; but such were not the grounds of their disagreement with the Church. The Puritans objected to certain ceremonial usages enjoined by the Act of Uniformity, 1559, and to episcopal government. Their case is stated fairly by Lord Bacon in the " Advertisement touching the controversies of the Church of England," 1589.

" On their part who call for Reformation, was first propounded some dislike of certain ceremonies supposed to be superstitious, some complaint of dumb ministers who possess rich benefices, and some invectives against the idle and monastical continuance within the Universities by those who had livings to be resided upon, and such like abuses. Thence they went on to condemn the Government of Bishops as a hierarchy remaining to us of the corruption of the Roman Church, and to sundry institutions as not sufficiently delivered from the pollution of former times. And lastly they advanced to define of an only and perpetual policy in the Church, which, without consideration of possibility or foresight of peril or perturbation of the Church and State, must be erected and planted by the magistrate. Here they stay, others, not being able to keep footing in so steep a ground, descend further. That the same must be entered into, accepted of the people at their peril, without the attending of the establishment of authority ; and in the meantime they refuse to communicate with us as reputing us to have no Church."

The cause behind these objections was the fear of a return to Rome : and behind this again the reason which is claimed to be the vindication of Puritan separation from the Church. According to Dr. Dale, who in Arnold's time, we must remember, was one of its recognised leaders, Nonconformity's central doctrine is the immediate relationship of the regenerate soul to God.

" He is akin to God through a supernatural birth, and is a partaker of the Divine Nature. All interference between himself and God, he resents. He can speak to God face to face."—(" Essays and Addresses," p. 250.)

He claims that this is the same principle as Luther's in the Reformation : that one aspect of it is the common element in Calvinism and

Arminianism, and that it was a fear of endangering this truth which made the Puritans condemn such ceremonial usages as altars, priestly vestments and Bishops. Dr. Dale challenges Arnold's statement that the Puritans tried to fix the Church to Calvinistic doctrine. This, at any rate, is unquestioned, that in the reign of Elizabeth attempts were made unsuccessfully to establish Calvinism in the Church. For example, Archbishop Whitgift issued the Nine Articles drawn up by the Lambeth Conference and containing definite statements of Calvinistic doctrine. These articles were withdrawn by order of Elizabeth. Dr. Dale points to Whitgift's action as showing a tendency to Calvinism in the Church ; while Arnold cites Elizabeth's action to show that because of the larger spirit of the Church, Calvinism, which the Puritans held, never could get established.

With regard to the second fact adduced by Arnold, that at the Hampton Court Conference of 1604 the Puritan party proposed the re-establishment of the Lambeth Articles, this, Dr. Dale admits, but with the qualifying statement that " the Puritan demand was chiefly for relaxation in the stringency of regulations touching rites and ceremonies."

The third article of evidence is undoubted and conclusive, that the Puritans complained before the Committee of the House of Lords in 1641, and that

Calvinistic doctrines were being preached against.

The fourth article is that at the Savoy Conference of 1661 the Puritan party wished to alter the Prayer Book so as to state their Calvinistic doctrine. The Bishops refused. Dr. Dale says that the Puritan demand was for greater detail in the specification of sins at Confession. Also he points out that Baxter and his friends admitted their agreement with the doctrines of the Church. To these counter facts it must be said that one of the details which the Puritans required to be inserted in the Confession was a clear expression of original sin. This however, is certain, that notwithstanding these attempts in 1604, 1641, and 1661, to introduce Calvinism into the formal statements of Church doctrine, yet we know that the Puritans felt themselves to be in agreement with the Church on matters of doctrine. For this fact Baxter and the trust deeds of early Presbyterian Chapels and the "Heads of Agreement" of 1691 between Presbyterians and Independents, are good witness. In addition there is Lord Bacon's "Advertisement touching the controversies of the Church of England" (1589), which we have quoted already.

The explanation is that there must have been in the Church a strong Calvinistic tendency. We know that there was a distinct Calvinistic party. The second and third Archbishops of Elizabeth's reign, Grindal and Whitgift, were both Calvinists.

There was a remarkable illustration of the two elements within the Church in the fact that Hooker preached at the Temple in the morning and Walter Travers in the evening. Of this incident it was said that "the forenoon sermon spoke Canterbury, the afternoon Geneva." Puritanism doubtless in the main was Calvinistic, and did attempt to make Calvinism the formal doctrine of the Church, but failed. It was a victory of the truer doctrine, rather than conscious resistance to a narrowing tendency. Arnold's facts are accurate, but in so far as he does not notice the prominent influence of Calvinism within the Church, he does not give a full and complete historical view. We say again that the advocacy of Calvinistic doctrine was not confined to the Puritans. On this point Dr. Dale is probably nearer to the truth than Arnold. Rightly to judge a movement one must see its central aim and how far it has succeeded in reaching it. Puritanism, no doubt, has emphasized and insisted on Calvinistic tenets, and has thereby hindered its own development ; but Calvinistic tenets had only a secondary place in its purpose, which was to bring the soul face to face with God.

From the origin of Puritanism we come to Arnold's view of the present state of Puritan theology.

To the strict and orthodox dissenter Arnold's

statement of the theology of Dissent will probably seem to be entirely praise. Sixty-one years have passed since " St. Paul and Protestantism " was written ; and during that time Nonconformity has adhered strictly to the Evangelical presentment of St. Paul's doctrine. It has held to this while the Church has been sliding into Unitarianism on one side and into Ritualism on another. From any widespread declension in doctrine up to now, Nonconformity has kept itself free. Recently, however, a widespread change has appeared. The change is in the use of words, a transformation of ideas without an alteration in the terms used. To take the instance of the doctrine of God. It is now simply a sign, a formula which can be used in whatever way the speaker likes; the definite and the Absolute have passed. Take the doctrine of the Atonement, once so distinctive in the Nonconformist presentation—what agreement on it is there now ? The signs which Arnold discerned in 1869 have become fulfilled. Still, so far as it has been rigid in doctrine it has justified Arnold's statements. Then he praised the elasticity of the Church, and doubtless it is elastic ; he opposed the rigidity of Nonconformity on its cardinal points, and rigid it certainly has been.

But how different now ! Calvinism went first and slowly. Now the old terms of justification, atonement, sin are disappearing, and the emphasis of preaching is laid less and less upon individual salvation and more and more upon the collective application of Christian principles. The Baptists and Congregationalists have always been receptive of new ideas; but even the strict Wesleyans are being touched by the Zeit Geist. As test cases, one might take the doctrine of inspiration and the doctrine of eternal punishment, and see how far Nonconformist theology of to-day has moved away from that of 1869. The point is that doctrinal discipline is less rigid than it used to be : that within the borders of Nonconformity there is greater scope for development than Arnold saw in the Nonconformity of his day; whereas, on the other hand, there is constant and increasing complaint of the laxity of doctrine prevalent in the Established Church, a laxity which, it is asserted, has led to Ritualism and Romanism and hence the crisis which has come recently upon the Church.

Arnold's criticism that Dissent was not in the main current of the national life, that it lacked centrality and was never filled with the sense of the historic life of the nation, becomes less and less true. In 1851 Arnold was appointed Inspector of Wesleyan and British Schools (chiefly Independent) and remained so for twenty years. His assistant for 18 years was Mr. Thomas Healing who is a well-known Wesleyan, and held office in that denomination. Mr. Healing, of all people, was

brought closely into contact with Arnold in that
best place for the observation of men, daily work.
Yet it is Mr. Healing who wrote in the *Methodist
Times*, January 23rd 1896, a reply to Mr.
Watkinson's complaints of Arnold's unfairness
and vulgarity ! Mr. Healing points out the friendship with Dr. Stoughton, whom Arnold introduced
into the Athenæum Club, Dr. Allon, Dr. Martineau,
the Rev. S. Martin and the Rev. W. Tyler. Arnold
was always seeking knowledge and experience.
Dr. Jenkins, one of the most distinguished of
the Wesleyan pastorate, makes the interesting
statement that he saw Arnold at one of Messrs.
Moody and Sankey's services, his tall figure
standing by their side, when Mr. Moody's
subject was " Blood " from Genesis to Revelation.
To this may be added the fact that on the morning
of the Sunday of his death, he attended Dr. Watson's
(Ian Maclaren) Church in Liverpool. Here are
Dr. Watson's words :

" It was Sacrament morning and I preached on
'The Shadow of the Cross.' We afterwards sang
the hymn 'When I survey the wondrous Cross.'
Mr. Arnold left before the Communion and went home.
As he came downstairs to lunch a servant heard him
saying softly to himself the first lines of the hymn.
At lunch Mr. Arnold spoke of the hymn, which he said
was the finest in the English language. Afterwards
he went out and in ten minutes he was dead ! "

But " St. Paul and Protestantism " contained other matter besides the criticism of the Nonconformist spirit. It gave a true and beautiful interpretation of St. Paul, which passed quickly into the religious world, and placed Arnold, layman as he was, among the best renderers of the Pauline ideas. His view of St. Paul was formative, as he would have said ; it was not mere intellectual analysis; there is insight ; there is edification in it. Arnold is so much before us as a critic that we miss the devotional side of his work.

When " St. Paul and Protestantism " was published in 1870 it secured immediate attention, and a second edition appeared the same year. Comments and reviews appeared from all directions. Then the general interest aroused stimulated Arnold to further work. We find him at this time, 23rd December 1871, reading in his mother's Bible every day and learning Hebrew. In the *Cornhill Magazine* of July and October 1871, appeared the first portions of matter which must have been composed during the Franco-Prussian War and afterwards became his famous work " Literature and Dogma." It was published in 1873 and went at once through three editions. It called forth a number of reviews to which Arnold replied in a series of articles printed in the *Contemporary Review* between October 1874 and September 1875. These were published with the title " God

and the Bible," and contain the principal contribution of Arnold to religious thought. " Literature
and Dogma " has puzzled minds of orthodox cast.
It abandons the whole of supernatural religion, yet
is suffused with a real and deep religious sense;
making claim to strengthen religion, it is said,
by some people, to overthrow it. The explanation
lies in Arnold's combination of the spirit of Voltaire
with that of a bishop. Rejected as pure Atheism
by some, " Literature and Dogma " has been a
light in darkness to others. It has led them through
a wholesome criticism towards the possibilities of
a new working conception of Christianity. Stirring
the keenest resentment on one hand, it has on the
other hand won the admiration of many younger
minds. Some attention may well be given to the
scope of the book. Like all Arnold's work it
concentrates on one or two main themes, expounds
them, moves round them, returns to them again,
and reiterates the formula which holds them.

The first theme of the book is the Israelitish
conception of God as the " Eternal Power not ourselves which makes for righteousness ; " or, in
scientific form, God is " the stream of tendency by
which all things seek to fulfil the law of their
being ; " and the false accretions to this conception
which found expression in the Messianic idea.

The second theme is the new statement of religion
given by Jesus in what Arnold called " the secret

and method of Jesus "; the accretions of the
first disciples and then later the Protestant and
Catholic Aberglaube—Aberglaube being defined
by Arnold as extra belief, poetry. The order
of thought is religion given, *aberglaube* invading.
Arnold's purpose is to strip the pure conception of
God, and the secret and method of Jesus, from
Aberglaube. These are the main themes illustrated
by many happy Biblical selections, accompanied by
original descriptions coming from the ordered and
lucid mind that Arnold had, and sometimes a
precision which was almost too precise, as when he
allots three-quarters of life to conduct, one-eighth
to art, and one eighth to intellect.

Then there are examinations of the arguments
for supernatural Christianity ; for prophecy and
miracles ; and for the New Testament records.
This part is negative, literary and naturalistic
criticism, aimed at showing the imperfection of our
records of Jesus. The originality of Arnold's
line is in the combination of critical results
with the religious spirit which infuses the
work. There is in it the same historical
and national sense as that of his father, and far
removed from the narrow outlook of the Evangelical
school. From the literary point of view
" Literature and Dogma," by its unerring selections
of scripture, its varied vocabulary, its satire, and
its approbation of orthodox witness, is rich in

beauty. Passages in it there are of solemn phrasing, such as that beginning "Poor Israel! Poor ancient people." Arnold's rendering of the Israelitish religion must always be regarded as a personal interpretation. In view of the uncertainties disclosed by criticism it is impossible to mark precisely the evolution of which Arnold speaks. Impossible surely it is to say that under Abraham or under Moses this or that change took place. Hence we cannot regard "Literature and Dogma" as religious history, but its rendering of Israelitish ideas has undeniable truths. And above all, critical conclusions, novel then, were made known and popular and acceptable.

"Literature and Dogma" was published in 1873, and in the same month went into a third edition. Numerous critical notices appeared. Arnold replied to some of these in a series of articles in the *Contemporary Review*, from October 1874, to September 1875, under the title "Review of objections to Literature and Dogma." These were published together as "God and the Bible." This therefore is complementary to "Literature and Dogma," and carries further Arnold's views of religion. He himself thought that "God and the Bible" contained some of his best prose. About one-half of the book is occupied with the Bible Canon and with Baur's theory that the fourth Gospel was written about A.D. 170 to help the anti-Jewish party. Arnold rejected Baur's theory and suggested that the fourth Gospel was written at Ephesus by a Greek Christian in the old age of John, whose sayings are incorporated in it. The first half of the book is a reply to certain reviewers of " Literature and Dogma." The criticisms with which Arnold dealt were :

1. That the first Israelitish conception of God was a crude Jahveh worship and not the revelation of righteousness as described by Arnold.
2. That the evolutionary explanation of the moral faculties necessarily destroys the theory of the Israelitish intuition of righteousness.
3. That religion is a matter of faith and cannot be grounded in experience.
4. That the anthropomorphic elements in Israel's conception of God prevent us from accepting the orthodox origin of the Israelitish conception of religion.

The technical details of literary criticism which take up so much of " God and the Bible," and its secondary character as being a reply to critics, make it rather less known than " Literature and Dogma." Arnold's own opinion of it we have seen. In a general depreciation of Arnold's religious writings Professor Saintsbury makes fun of Arnold's arguments from the roots, " as," " bhu," " sta," yet pushing home definitions and reducing familiar or impressive formulæ to simple terms is valuable. What is puzzling is Arnold's assumption of orthodoxy while laying down most destructive principles. That is Arnold's manner ; it goes with him. What is sound and permanent in " God and the Bible " and " Literature and Dogma " is the sure ground upon which he bases religion. The most recent trend of Christian apologetics is in line with Arnold, in this respect ; the defence is founded upon human experience, the historical witness, the pragmatic confirmation. When these books were published the critical movement was rising, was constantly changing, was apparently threatening religion and the moral life itself. Arnold's influence gave a new set to the critical movement. Now, nearly sixty years later, it is possible to measure the movement in all directions, and to see how much of it has been established, how much rebutted. The Church changed still lives. But one movement has died, and that is the avowedly anti-religious movement known as Free Thought. It may be said truly that Arnold's influence undermined it.

In 1872, between the production of the articles in the *Cornhill* which was the nucleus of "Literature and Dogma," and their publication in complete form, Arnold produced " A Bible Reading for Schools," as a kind of illustration of the principles

of " Literature and Dogma." This consisted of
an introduction and Arnold's own translation of
Chapters 40 to 66 of Isaiah. Later he issued for
adults an edition of the same, adding such other
portions as were connected with the subject.
Arnold sent a copy to Cardinal Newman; it was
acknowledged in a letter from the Cardinal, May
24 1872, and was followed by a letter from
Arnold to Newman, four days later. In that letter
Arnold stated that he had learnt his habits, methods,
and ruling ideas from four people, Wordsworth,
Goethe, Sainte-Beuve and Newman. The whole correspondence, bringing together the two outstanding
figures in religious thought of the Victorian period,
forms a fascinating picture of two personalities so
near, so far. Unfortunately the letters are not in
Mr. Russell's collection, but were first published
in the *Times Literary Supplement*, March 10 1921
and March 31 1921. In April and May 1883, in
the *Nineteenth Century*, he published " Isaiah of
Jerusalem." In the same year with these articles
as an introduction, he published Chapters 1 to
39 of Isaiah, with the text of the Authorised Version.
These two editions of Isaiah are not well known;
yet they are pure Arnold. We have to remember
that neither of the revised parts of the Bible had
been issued ; that of the New Testament came in
1881, and of the Old Testament in 1885. In
Arnold's first part, Chapters 40 to 66, principles of

translation to be applied to Hebrew Literature are
laid down, as convincingly as in the Homer Lectures.
Alterations where necessary for elucidating meanings,
moderation in innovations, careful preservation
of the beauty of the Authorised Version, these
are the main lines of treatment.

The other portion of " Isaiah of Jerusalem "
comes in between the publication of the Revised
New Testament and the Revised Old Testament.
Arnold prints the Authorised Version in this case,
with his own notes. The introduction is of a
different kind from that of his first book. He
proposes two necessities for the understanding of the
situation ; and it is to this latter that Arnold devoted
his attention. He elucidates the situation by comparing that group of nations with a similar group
at the time he was writing, and this gave him a
chance for his humour. Napoleon as Sennacherib,
Austria as Egypt, France as Assyria : this was
all happy and effective.

In " God and the Bible " Arnold acknowledged
that the ideas of " Literature and Dogma " were
suggested to his mind by reading Bishop Butler.
In January 1876, he gave two lectures entitled
" Bishop Butler and the Zeit-Geist," at the Edin-
burgh Philosophical Institution. These Lectures
were printed in the *Contemporary Review*, February
and March, 1876. They have the manner of the
" Essays in Criticisms," the manner of the Sainte-

Beuve causeries, just the biographical touch which illumines the subject, just the same sure placing, just the same felicities of opening and closing. After finishing " Literature and Dogma " and " God and the Bible," he turned to foundation work suggested by the Analogy and the Sermons. Thus in these essays we get a statement, and almost the only statement, of the scientific and the philosophical grounds of his beliefs. The assumptions which lie at the root of Arnold's work are here discussed. The reader who is familiar with Arnold will know how he assumed the popular manner, an air of stating the proved and indisputable, while really taking sides in highly contested propositions. For example, on religious matters he concealed the assumptions and reasoning on which his views rested and calmly stated as an universal judgment most disputed premises. The position which he assumed is only tenable by admitting the conclusions of the naturalistic school of Science. In the " Butler Essays " Arnold reaches the scientific and philosophical bases of the arguments. He reasons about them instead of merely stating the conclusions of the cultivated world in general.

" Butler on Instincts " is a fair example. According to Butler's scheme of things the human instincts were planted in man of set design to produce certain courses of action; that the Conscience arbitrates between them, and uses them for

their right end ; that self-love is one out of many
affections ; that one and the other of these instincts
are designed to supplement the others. Arnold
replied that there is a certain correspondence between
this theory of nature and the facts but that we have
to go to the origin of these instincts and affections.
Yet Butler's appeal to experience, and the great
argument drawn from the actual facts of life, com-
mended itself to Arnold. The impressive conclusions of Butler are heard sounding through all
Arnold's work.

In the month following the appearance of the
second and last of Butler's articles Arnold
published in *Macmillan's Magazine*, April 1876,
the text of an address to London clergy given at
Sion College. Considering the kind of thing which
Arnold had already written something must be said
in praise of the liberal minds of the clergy who
invited him. The address is a statement of Arnold's
idea of the Church as a natural society for the
promotion of goodness, not an institution for the
propagation of tenets of belief. He said that the
Church has a duty to bring about a great social
renewal. And then in his natural manner he
turns on the Dissenters. The Disestablishment
campaign was then just beginning under the
influence of Birmingham Radicalism. Arnold attacked the spirit and temper of the Nonconformists
and said that the new generation would turn away

from the political attack as soon as the real mission of the Church was realised. Disestablishment apparently is as far off as ever, but not for the reason that he gave. The address shows Arnold's loyalty to the Church, his natural and undeniable love for its historic character, shows once more his abiding desire to change the Church, so as to restore its function as a natural and national institution. The really curious note in the address is the democratic one. The Church is to have the sympathy of the masses. It is the same strain as that in the Equality article of " Mixed Essays," the same that produced " Literature and Dogma " and the definitions of Culture. Aristocratic and exclusive as he was, there is always to be noted in him the sense of the general good. The picture of Dr. Dale practising as the brilliant pugilist with Mr. Chamberlain in Birmingham exactly preserves the spirit of the period. There is a beautiful and personal conclusion to the article; he has the sense of growing old, and feels the need for making progress in grace and peace.

A kind of epilogue to this address appeared in the article " A Last Word on the Burials Bill." It deals with a subject of strife now forgotten. The circumstances which produced the article have passed but in having his word on them Arnold laid down certain principles of public worship which may well be emphasized. In considering

the question of the service at Burial he was brought
into contact with the whole question of Public
Worship.   Here comes the opportunity for the
sure judgment of taste; what bears a public
character should be done and said worthily.   No one
will say that the common Englishman glides at once
and by nature into a strain pure, noble and elevated.
The sects have not the right each to produce and
use their own service.   What bars the right,
is the higher right of the community.

We cannot go with him in the argument that,
just because the Anglican Church is the National
Church, therefore its services provide the medium
and reasonable service for public use.   But we
can go with him in the exercise of his judgment
as to what is fine and worthy, and we are
with him in his estimate of the grandeur of the
Burial Service of the Prayer Book.   Arnold praised
the Catholic service for the dead, and suggested
a new revision of the reading from the 15th Corin-
thians and the addition of the Ezekiel prophecy of
the Valley of Dry Bones.   Here Arnold left the
subject of Dissent and the Church ;   but his work on
religious subjects was not yet finished.   An article,
" A Psychological Parallel," was published in the
Contemporary Review of November 1876.   The
old questions, the imperfection of human witness,
the misunderstanding of the disciples and of St.
Paul, the superstitions of great men—these were the

themes. Taken as a whole, and especially the preface, "Last Essays" shows that the need for a scientific statement of Christianity was gaining on Arnold more and more. The Butler articles show him treating religion on its psychological side. Thus the question arises : had Arnold lived long enough what would have been his attitude as the scientific movement gradually increased.

By 1876 Arnold had completed his connected work on religion. Seven years later in 1883 came the "Isaiah of Jerusalem" volume of which we have already spoken. In April 1887 in the *Nineteenth Century*, he published under the title "A Friend of God," a review of "The Following of Christ," by John Tauler, translated into English by J. R. Morell, which he had been reading while on his visit to America. The interest of the article is mainly personal in that it shows Arnold still deeply marked by ethical ideals, still retaining his interest in the inward character of religion. He likes in Tauler "the golden single sentences," finding them to be a possession for the mind and soul, fitted to form the character. Such is the last sound, on the solemn themes which most interested Arnold, of his voice, grave and wise, and appealing from his generation to ours.

MATTHEW ARNOLD: A CRITIC OF
THE VICTORIAN PERIOD

By Charles H. Harvey

An attempt to set forth the comprehensive range of Arnold's influence,
an influence which has touched modern life at many points with disturbing force. An internal view of
the Victorians is presented to the
reader. "As we recede from the last
century, and its historical features become clearer, we see that Matthew
Arnold, inside the Victorian era, was
the Victorian critic." (Preface)